Basic Asian

in the kitchen

yang

and

for yin

you need

Everything

D1404267

Cornelia Schinharl   Sebastian Dickhaut   Kelsey Lane

Basic Asian Contents

Front Flap: Basic Overview of Asian Regional Cuisines
Back Flap: What Type of Asian Cook Are You?

Asian
cuisine will get you!

It's Everywhere.

When we think *Basic Asian* we think authentic, wise, peaceful, colorful, loud, raw and wild. So much to internalize. But when it really comes down to it, it can be as simple, bright and white as rice in a mother-of-pearl bowl.

Asian cuisine can bowl you over, either in a single blow as it catapults you to the Canton market where ducks quack and shrimp sizzles in a wok or with a soft caress like the waves along the Java coast in Indonesia where you can sit and eat papaya while dipping your toes in the water. Asian cuisine will get you, whether it's in a sushi bar, a teahouse or a coffee shop. Its spirit is everywhere. So where should we begin in this book?

Right where you are—at home. Where a wok is already waiting, where you can buy green onions and garlic just around the corner—plus ginger and soy sauce without going too far. This is enough to initiate you into Asian cooking, which is not so much a matter of Zen and the exotic as it is of fresh ingredients and harmony in the preparation. This is a project that has engaged the efforts of farmer's wives, palace chefs and scholars for centuries. *Basic Asian* will explain it in such a way that someone from any culture can understand it. We'll tell you all about Asian-style shopping and cooking while supplying you with authentic recipes adapted for Western kitchens. Not a random hodgepodge, but clearly defined lines, as light as a Zen garden and as dazzling as a chile pepper.

On top of all this, it's healthy and can even bring some order into your life. But first let's get a general overview and the rest will follow naturally.

basic

"Help!
All I Can Find is
the Strawberry Yogurt!"

"Light, dark, sweet soy sauce; red, green, yellow curry paste; hundred-year-old eggs, soba, dried seaweed, udon, galangal, kaffir limes, bok choy... Help! Please! I only wanted to do a little Asian cooking and now I'm lost in the market jungle. How can I get out of here without starving? I'll never make it!"

You don't think so?

Try to imagine it from someone else's perspective. Imagine a rural Chinese person who is visiting the United States—they're shopping in a Western super-market for the very first time. What's all this milk, buttermilk, strawberry yogurt? To us it's a walk in the park because we grew up with these products, just as the Chinese grew up with hundred-year-old eggs. But we are lucky in one respect—at least we're familiar with curry, soy and limes—so the Asian market jungle isn't as bad as you might think. Think of it as an expedition to the exotic food shelves.

It'll be a walk in the park in no time.

Exotic Shopping

Five Golden Rules for Successfully Navigating an Asian Market

The other day before making dinner I said to myself, "Okay, I'll take the plunge into Asian cuisine by making spring rolls, since I've already had them and know what I'm supposed to end up with. I've written out my shopping list. I already have sugar, salt and oil for deep-frying. I can buy chile peppers, garlic, green onions, chives, shrimp and limes at the supermarket, and maybe even cellophane noodles and some fish sauce."

"So, now I've got all that straight. What else do I need? Spring roll pastry, rice vinegar, hot chile oil. These might be harder to find. Let me think... I might find them at Mr. Li's Hong Kong Asian Market. I'll go there next."

Rule no. 1

Start with what you know. The first step is always the most important so don't make the steps too high. Then the climb won't seem so difficult.

Rule no. 2

Be aware of where you are and where you need to go. If you're in a large city, go to your favorite Asian market, whether this involves several small specialists or one large, well-stocked store. If you're in a small town, you'll seldom have a choice of markets but try your best to find one with quality ingredients. If you're out in the country, fill up your basic Asian pantry either when you happen to visit a large city or by mail order (you might also find some ingredients at health-food stores) and then use whatever fresh ingredients you can get your hands on—in the true spirit of Asian cooking!

"So I finally found the market. Look at all the colors! This shelf of bottles is pure pop-art. What could they possibly contain? Wok chefs would know but I'm no pharmacist. Back there by the rice sacks it looks a little chaotic. Oops! I almost knocked over that stack of cans. And what's this? Egg shells? Oh, hundred-year eggs, well, um, now what did I come here for?"

Rule no. 3

Live in the moment. Stick your nose into everything Asian, take in the vibrant colors and listen to the sounds, feel its healing powers and taste its secrets, accept both the order and the chaos, but don't lose your head!

"Now I have almost everything. I just need light rice vinegar. Hmmm, I can only find the dark. Light would be better. What do you think, Mr. Li? Do you happen to have a bottle hidden away for gourmets? I'd love to have it!"

"Oh, I see you also have green onions, Mr. Li. Why are you taking them away? They're too old? Okay, I'll get some at my produce market. Do you think they'll also have chives? Do you have any? And what's in that bottle? Chrysanthemum wine, I see. I might as well try that, too." And now, may the appetite be with you.

They'll tell you if you should use green onions from your produce market for your spring rolls rather than their own that have been sitting around too long. Another piece of advice: every time you go shopping, buy something you've never had before and experiment with it at home. And finally: be good to Mr. Li and he'll be good to you.

Rule no. 4

Ask, ask, ask! This is the only way you'll learn. And demonstrate your wisdom by asking with humility. That will win you respect—as well as better ingredients.

Rule no. 5

Build on your experience. This is the only way to go beyond the familiar. Mr. Li is a person from a country where cooking and eating mean everything, every day, including holidays. And since they do this for a living, they know a lot about ingredients and will be glad to share their knowledge. So assume that the people in the Asian market know better than anyone else what's good.

Basics in the Asian Pantry

The Beginner Track—Expandable from Size S to XL

Everything you need for Asian cuisine, from the starting gate to the winner's circle, but don't usually keep in your pantry:

If you want to cook Asian food, one option is to look no further than your local produce market or farmer's market. You'll be going there every day, just like the Thai cook goes to the vegetable market, because freshness is the most important ingredient in Asian cuisine. But how does the Thai cook manage to chop all the ingredients for the wok? And how will you manage it? First of all, you can use ready-made products for your sauces. That's right, soy sauce, miso paste, coconut milk, nori sheets—all prepared products that get their uniqueness from fine seasonings.

Since you won't need *all* these prepared products right off the bat, we've developed an expandable set of staples. Size S is for those who know almost nothing about Asian cuisine. It can be expanded to size M for those who want to know more, to L for Asian cooking fanatics who know exactly what they want and XL for those who must learn absolutely everything.

However, although a bottle of soy sauce or can of coconut milk would be gone in a second in an Asian kitchen, it usually takes us a little longer. So try buying smaller quantities and don't leave anything in an open can but transfer it to another container so it'll stay fresh longer.

Size S is for "Standard"

Aromatic rice: Standard side dish. Dry rice stored in an airtight container in a dark place will keep for up to 6 months.

Chile sauce, sweet: More for dipping than for cooking. Good in salad dressing. Once opened, will keep in the refrigerator for at least 1 year. For homemade chile sauce, see page 57.

Coconut milk: Transfer leftover to another container, refrigerate and use within 1 week. Or freeze and keep for months. For homemade coconut milk, see page 147.

Fish sauce: Once opened, will keep in the refrigerator for 1 year.

Noodles for standard dishes: For example, dry Chinese egg noodles for wok stir-fries keep for 1 year in an airtight container in a dark place.

Palm sugar: This sap of special Asian palms that is reduced and dried has a caramel-licorice flavor. It's great in dips with fish sauce or sauces made with coconut milk. When stored in an airtight container, it keeps almost forever. Use interchangeably in recipes that call for brown sugar.

Rice vinegar: Made from fermented rice wine. Choose the one you want, either dark or light. Dark is aged longer, which makes it more aromatic than the light. Japanese rice vinegar is often sweeter than Chinese. Substitutions: Sherry vinegar or apple cider vinegar, thinned with a little water if necessary.

Rice wine (sake, mirin): Once opened, keeps in the refrigerator for 1 year.

Sesame oil: Once opened, keeps in the refrigerator for 6 months.

Soy sauce, all-purpose: Once opened, refrigerate and try to use within 2–3 months (the taste changes quickly).

Spices: Coriander, cumin, turmeric, cloves, nutmeg and anise are the basics that can also be used for making curry powder or curry paste (see page 109; otherwise use a prepared mixture to start). Whole seasonings will keep in airtight containers in a dark place for 1 year; ground for 6 months.

Tea for every day: Depending on your preference, try green tea or black tea from China, India or Sri Lanka. It's better to buy it in a tea shop or organic market rather than in an Asian market—the quality will be higher, the more specialized the store. Sealed in an airtight container and stored in a dark place, tea keeps for 1–2 months.

Size M is for "Musts"

Basmati rice: Long-grain rice served with Indian dishes. Dry rice stored in an airtight container in a dark place keeps for up to 6 months.

Bean sauce, black: Made of fermented soybeans; used for marinades and very strong sauces. Can be spiced up with chiles. Once opened, keeps in the refrigerator for 6 months.

Cardamom: Green or brown pods (dried fruit of the plant) with sweet, aromatic seeds. Pods or seeds are crushed; seeds can also be ground. Stored in an airtight container in a dark place, pods keep for 1 year and powder keeps for 6 months.

Curry paste, red: Keeps almost forever (definitely more than 1 year). Refrigerate after opening. For homemade curry paste, see page 109.

Dashi, instant: Japanese stock made from seaweed and bonito flakes (cured and dried tuna) that should be added to near-boiling water. Keeps almost forever (definitely

10

more than 1 year). For homemade dashi stock, see page 59.

Dried mushrooms: For example, shiitake. Stored in an airtight container in a dry, dark place, they keep for at least 1 year; after soaking, they keep in the refrigerator for 3 days.

Ginger, Japanese pickled: Once opened, keeps in the refrigerator for about 1 month. For homemade pickled ginger, see page 39.

Kecap manis: Sweet soy sauce from Indonesia. Refrigerate after opening and try to use within 2–3 months.

Lentils, red: Stored in an airtight container in a dark place, they keep for at least 1 year.

Mango chutney: A sweet and sour, spicy-hot paste made from cooked mangos. Good as a condiment and as a dip. Once opened, keeps in the refrigerator for about 2–3 months. For homemade mango chutney, see page 75.

Mirin: Sweet Japanese rice wine used for cooking. Once opened, keeps in the refrigerator for 3 months.

Miso paste, medium-dark: Once opened, keeps in the refrigerator for at least 1 year.

Noodles for special dishes: For example, wheat, cellophane (mung bean) or rice noodles. Stored in an airtight container in a dark place, they keep for 1 year.

Nori sheets: Paper-thin sheets of dried, compressed seaweed. Today they're almost always roasted and seasoned. Used for making handmade sushi rolls. Once opened, store in an airtight container in a dry place and try to use within 1 week.

Oyster sauce: Concentrated sweet and salty sauce made from oyster juice and caramel. Better for cooking than for dipping. Once opened, keeps in the refrigerator for 1 year.

Sambal: Indonesian/Malaysian seasoning sauce made from chile peppers used as a table condiment. Sambal oelek is spicy-hot. Sambal manis is sweet and not too hot. Once opened, these keep in the refrigerator for at least 1 year. For homemade sambals, see page 89.

Sesame seeds: Stored in an airtight container in a dark place, they keep for about 6 months.

Sichuan pepper: Stored in an airtight container in a dark place, whole peppercorns keep for at least 1 year, ground peppercorns for 6 months.

Spring roll pastry: You can buy this frozen in sheets that are about 4-inch x 4-inch, about 8-inch x 8-inch and 12-inch x 12-inch. Carefully remove the individual sheets from the package and cover with a damp cloth until you're ready to use them. Re-freeze the rest.

Star anise: Stored in an airtight container in a dark place, whole anise keeps for 1 year; ground for 6 months.

Tamarind paste: Keeps in the refrigerator for at least 1 year.

Tea, Japanese: Almost always green. Stored in an airtight container in a dark place, this keeps for 1–2 months.

Wasabi: From a tube or in powdered form for stirring into liquid, wasabi keeps for 2–3 months refrigerated.

Size L is for "Luxurious"

Beans, black: Fermented soybeans added to dishes whole or reduced in a sauce. Once opened, transfer to another container, refrigerate and use within 1–2 weeks.

Beer, Asian: Once opened, hopefully keeps no more than 15 minutes.

Chickpeas: Store the dry variety of this legume in an airtight container and they'll keep for over a year.

Curry paste, green: Keeps almost forever (definitely more than 1 year). Refrigerate after opening. For homemade curry paste, see page 109.

Five-spice powder: Chinese spice blend. Stored in an airtight container in a dark place, it keeps for 6 months.

Garam masala: Indian spice blend which varies like curry powder but unlike curry is typically comprised without turmeric. Stored in an airtight container in a dark place, it keeps for 6 months.

Hoisin sauce: Sweet and spicy Chinese sauce made from fermented soybeans, chile peppers, garlic and sesame oil. Good as a marinade or dip. Refrigerate after opening and try to use within 2–3 months.

Miso paste, light: Once opened, keeps in the refrigerator for at least 1 month.

Noodles for fanatics: For example, dried udon and soba. Stored in an airtight container in a dark place, they keep for 1 year.

Rice paper: Very fragile, so be careful not to bend it. Stored in an airtight container, it keeps for well over a year, or more.

Saffron: Dried stigmas from a specific crocus blossom. Stored in an airtight container in a dark place, the threads keep for 6 months, and ground saffron keeps for 2 months.

Soy sauce, special: For example, light Chinese soy sauce. Refrigerate after opening and try to use within 2–3 months.

Sushi rice: Stored in an airtight container in a dark place, this keeps for up to 6 months.

Tamarind, compressed: Stored in an airtight container in a cool and dark place, keeps for over a year. You can also purchase tamarind paste, which needs to be refrigerated.

Size XL is for "Extra Lavish"

Bean paste, red: Sweetened paste made from azuki or kidney beans and used in desserts and baked goods. Once opened, transfer to another container, refrigerate and use within 1 year.

Curry paste, yellow: Keeps almost forever (definitely more than 1 year). Refrigerate after opening.

Flour, Asian: For example, rice or chickpea flours used for foods such as pakoras. Stored in an airtight container in a dark place, they keep for 1 year.

Seafood, dried: Stored in an airtight container in a dry and dark place, this keeps for 2 months.

Sticky rice: Dry rice stored in an airtight container in a dark place keeps for up to 6 months.

Wine, Asian: If you want it to be authentic, buy, for example, Great Wall brand (China) or Suntory brand (Japan). If you want to taste something good, drink sake, beer, tea or water.

For more information on **anise, chile peppers, cilantro, coconut milk, curry, dried products, fish sauce, ginger, miso, rice wine, sesame, soy sauce, tamarind** and **wasabi**, see pages 12–15 under "The Exotic 17."

For more information on rice, see page 16; for noodles, see page 17; for soy, see page 20.

You'll also find additional information on **beer** (page 127), **bean sauce** (page 102), **five-spice powder** (page 46), **rice wine** (page 75), **Sichuan pepper** (page 134), **tea** (page 39) and **wine** (page 109).

11

the
exotic
17
the
basic aromatic
flavors of
yin & yang

Rice Wine

On page 75 we'll describe whether rice wine is more like a beer or a liqueur. Here we're referring to its quality as a "seasoning," which means we're not talking about the finest types. Chinese rice wine is mainly brewed from soaked, glutinous rice and a little grain (wheat, millet) plus yeast or rice mold. Its color ranges from amber to medium-brown. It has a slightly smoky flavor, which means it goes well with meat and strong flavors. Japanese sake, similar but made solely from rice, is clearer and complements vegetables and fish. Mirin is sweetened sake used for cooking.

Garlic

Whether it's a Thai curry, Indian dal, Vietnamese wok dish, braised Chinese meat or Indonesian spring roll, it tastes only half as good without garlic. Along with ginger and green onions, garlic is one of the three magic seasonings that set the basic tone for many Asian dishes. Because of the typical Asian chef's sense of balance, its flavor is never distinct (in contrast to southern European cuisine). To achieve this balance, they counteract garlic's extreme pungency with the intense freshness of herbs or neutralize it with hearty meats or strong soy sauce.

Sesame

You'll experience a new kind of sesame flavor when you taste the dark oil of toasted sesame seeds. Can this possibly come from something that tastes so bland when sprinkled on hamburger buns? Yes it can, because toasting brings out the flavor. The light oil made from untoasted sesame seeds, which can be used for sautéing, has only a slight flavor that tastes nothing like sesame compared to the above-mentioned dark seasoning oil for dips, sauces, salads and marinades. Asian cooking also features light and black sesame seeds, sometimes toasted, used to garnish or flavor rice and noodle dishes, as well as desserts.

Cilantro

You might not fall in love with cilantro at first taste. Some people would gladly subscribe to the theory that this relative of parsley got its name (coriander) because it smells like bugs (Greek "koris"). But this aversion can quickly become an addiction. For beginners, add leaves to soups at the very end. For advanced culinarians, mix leaves with basil and mint in a salad. Fanatics might even chew cilantro leaves and root to stimulate digestion. Even the tiny dried seeds of the plant, coriander, serve as a seasoning. These seeds taste a little like orange peel and are widely used in curries.

Soy Sauce

Whether it's used as sushi dip, in dim sum or in a Thai salad, this salty soybean extract fermented with grain is almost a constant accompaniment to Asian meals. Light Chinese soy sauce is younger and saltier (for fish, light meat and noodle dishes) than the aged, aromatic dark type (for braising and dips). Japan's sauces are often milder and therefore good for a wide range of uses. Indonesian kecap manis is boiled down and thickened with palm sugar (for dips and marinades). Note that once opened, soy sauce decomposes and changes in taste, but not for the better, after 1–2 months. So try to purchase small bottles and use them up quickly.

Anise

A shot of the anise-flavored "pastis" before meals is to Provence what a snack of pan masala (betel leaf filled with anise and other spices) is to India—a pleasant stimulant for the digestion. Aniseeds originated in the Mediterranean region but also lend their refreshing spiciness to curries and vegetable dishes throughout Asia. Star anise, the sun-dried blossom of a magnolia, is authentically Asian and spicier than aniseed. In China, whole or crushed stars or seeds are used for flavoring braised meat, soups and desserts. Star anise is a component of China's five-spice blend, besides being used in some Provençal anise liqueurs.

Fish Sauce

This also takes some getting used to because the odor alone is enough to stop you in your tracks. It smells just like anchovies and shrimp mixed with salt and left out in the sun too long. But when you put just a little of this extract into soup, salads, dip or on fish and meat (really!), there's a flavor explosion that turns everything to pure gold. That's why Thai cooks pour their "nam pla" and the Vietnamese their milder "nuoc nam" onto everything that we would normally season with salt. If you have a choice, buy the lighter and more expensive fish sauce because, in this case, you do get what you pay for.

Dried Products

The scarcity of food and the desire to get as much as possible out of every ingredient has turned Asia's housewives and chefs into the world's best preservers. Their masterpieces are the dry products that store up flavor like dried mushrooms such as the shiitake (see photo), shrimp and anchovies for seasoning or pastes, bonito flakes (cured tuna shavings) for soup, seaweed such as kombu for dashi stock or wakame for miso soup. After soaking (soak mushrooms overnight in cold water and 1 hour in warm water; soak seaweed 1 hour in cold water), the soaking liquid from dried products is often filtered and used as well.

Wasabi

In Japan, where brooks babble most peacefully, is the home of one of the hottest culinary items in Asia. On the banks of these brooks grows the green wasabi root whose flavor is similar to horseradish and can sometimes taste like mustard. It takes 5 years to grow 8 inches long at which time the sushi masters can grate it on a rough sharkskin into a fine snowy condiment. Since Japanese stream beds aren't that common and sushi lovers can't wait forever, wasabi is also cultivated, grated and dried, then sold as a powder or made into a paste. It's not as good as the original but it's better than nothing!

Lemon Grass

Many people dream of learning to cook Southeast Asian cuisine, but few truly know what to do with the aromatic flavorant lemon grass. And this could be a real problem since Thai and Vietnamese cooks wouldn't dream of cooking without "citronelle." But if you begin using this seasoning (which is somewhere between an herb and a spice) in tiny increments, you'll end up a convert. Here are a few tips: Use only the bottom 4–8 inches and remove the hard outer leaves first; when simmering whole, pound flat (then remove before eating the dish); when frying in a wok, chop very finely (OK to eat).

Coconut Milk

The coconut palm supplies us with ladles, mats and wrappers for cooking, but the best gift to come from this tropical tree is coconut milk, made by pressing the liquid from grated coconut diluted with water. Just like cow's milk, acid makes it curdle and its cream rises to the top. This cream can then be used like butter for sautéing. The silky, exotic flavor of coconut milk is what makes the curries, soups, rice dishes and desserts of Southeast Asia so unique and secures it a place in the standard pantry. For homemade coconut milk, see page 147.

Chile Peppers

It's hard to believe Asia didn't have chiles until the Spanish and Portuguese brought them from America. That means there was no Thai curry paste and no Indonesian sambals. But today you can find chile peppers all across Asia, especially the Southeast. The smaller peppers are often hotter than the larger; the best can be nutty, bitter, fruity or have a citrus flavor. Red chiles have a fuller aroma than unripe green ones. Both are milder if you remove the seeds and rest of the interior. Always wear gloves when working with chiles, and don't touch your face. Also, wash your cutting board and knives well.

Miso

Since the world has taken so eagerly to sushi, we hope it also gives miso a chance. This Japanese paste made from fermented soybeans (usually with rice, less often alone or with barley) is not only wonderfully healthy but is also a delight for gourmets— for example, the way it can transform a dried fish and seaweed stock into the beguiling and refreshing miso soup. You can use miso in mayonnaise for dips and dressing, in a marinade for grilling and in a purée for sauces. Light shiro-miso paste is mild while the aged, dark aka-miso paste has a saltier, stronger taste. The medium-dark awase-miso paste has many uses.

the exotic 17

the basic aromatic flavors of yin & yang

Limes

America may have given Asia the chile pepper but the Far East gave the rest of the world the lime, which now adorns food and drinks globally. The lime doesn't care where it grows as long as it's really hot. In tropical Asia, limes are used in soups, curries, dressings, dips and marinades. They have more juice than their bigger yellow cousin, the lemon, and aren't as intensely sour; instead they provide more fragrance and a slight sweetness. The rind of the wrinkled kaffir lime is valued as a seasoning, as are the leaves which are often available fresh (which you can freeze for later), frozen or dried.

Ginger

No flavor is more Asian than ginger, which lends the final zing to both Indian curry and Japanese sushi. It combines the spiciness of chiles with the citrus flavor of limes, is a must in curry paste and with coconut milk, staves off nausea and colds and was once the second-most popular spice in the world after pepper. A favorite use today is to chop the fresh root finely and simmer to flavor entrées. The same can be done with its somewhat hotter and more bitter relative galangal. Tip: Freeze peeled ginger in foil and grate as needed. Or pickle it the way the Japanese do (see page 39).

Tamarind

True curries and chutneys often feature tamarind. Looking at the brown pods of the tamarind tree, you would never guess what they contain—a whole lot of sweet and sour with the sour predominating. This makes the pressed pulp and the paste produced from the fruit and pods a favorite Asian ingredient for adding a pleasant, sour taste to soup and other dishes. To add tamarind to dishes, soak 2 tablespoons of the pulp in $1/3$ cup warm water for 10 minutes, then press the mixture through a strainer, or use 1 tablespoon paste stirred into $1/3$ cup warm water. Use this liquid seasoning in Asian cooking.

Curry

The spice blend that Indian mariners once mixed together for eating "karis" on trips to and from Europe became the West's "curry." Sometimes in India you can find a pre-made basic curry spice mix (e.g., with coriander, cumin, pepper and chili powder) and with additional spices depending on the region. In Southeast Asia, these seasonings are mixed with onions, garlic, ginger or galangal and spiced sauces or pastes to make curry paste. The aromatic red paste is the most popular, followed by the fresh, tangy green. Check specialty stores for pre-made pastes, or for making homemade, see page 109.

Rice
Asian Style

The Asian equivalent of potatoes, noodles, bread and cereal all rolled into one.

In Asia, there aren't many recipes that call for it. And yet, Asian life revolves around it. Rice. It's present at every meal, quietly steaming in its bowl. Where the Western world would more typically be eating potatoes, noodles, bread, pizza or cereal, there usually would be only one choice in Asia: rice or something made from rice.

Nine out of ten grains of rice in the world come from the Far East, the home of the sweet "oryza sativa" grass. Most rice also stays there and, except for the Indian basmati, is usually prepared to be a little sticky so it can easily be eaten with chopsticks. This is as true of the long-grain Thai aromatic rice as it is of the round short-grain Japanese sushi rice—its stickiness has less to do with the shape of the grain than it does with the starch. For example, so much "glue" is produced when Vietnamese sticky rice is prepared that it can stick together like pudding. This is good for a dessert but bad for rice that's meant to retain its characteristic shape. In this case, steaming is better than boiling because it keeps the grains separate. Here's how the different methods work:

Boiling Rice

With this method, the rice boils in just enough liquid so that it will all be soaked up and the flavor and starch will remain in the grains. Some Asian cooks wash the rice before cooking to remove external starch residue. We've also tried boiling it without washing the rice first and haven't noticed any real difference, at least not with aromatic rice. But here's how it's done (including washing):

Swirl the aromatic rice around in a pot of cold water and strain. Repeat this procedure three or four times until the water remains clear. Cover rice with cold, unsalted water (2 cups water to 1 cup rice) and bring to a boil. Then cover and cook over the lowest possible heat for no more than 20 minutes. Fluff the rice with a fork and enjoy.

Steaming Rice

Steaming produces rice that separates easily into grains. In the case of aromatic basmati rice, it sometimes separates too easily to use chopsticks; if you use short- or medium-grain glutinous rice (such as Japanese rice), it turns out exactly right for making balls and dipping in sauce Southeast-Asian style. Here's how to do it:

Soak glutinous rice overnight in cold water. Drain and pour into a steamer lined with a damp cloth. Cover the steamer and fold the corners of the cloth over the top. Cover the pot and steam over boiling water for 30 minutes, fluff the grains and enjoy.

Rice Basics

Aromatic rice (photo bottom)
Long-grain rice from Southeast Asia with a fragrant aroma. Almost the only kind available is Thai aromatic rice (e.g., jasmine) as Thailand is the only major rice exporter in Asia.

Basmati rice (photo middle)
Long-grain rice from Northern India with an intoxicating, nutty aroma that cooks up light, fluffy and tender. Often sautéed before boiling. Cooking basmati rice: see page 76.

Glutinous rice
Medium-grain rice that releases its starch when cooked (mainly the protein amylopectin) so that the grains stick together, making this rice suitable for desserts: see page 150.

Sushi rice (photo top)
Round-grain rice from Japan that's ideal for shaping into sushi. Can also be served as a side dish with Teriyaki Duck (page 143), etc. You can substitute risotto rice. Cooking sushi rice: see page 53.

Noodle Basics

Buckwheat noodles (photo middle)

The buckwheat is supplemented with wheat flour (Japanese soba ranging from spaghetti-thin to linguini-thick) or potato starch (Korean naengmyon, thinner than soba). Both are parboiled and eaten both hot and cold, typically in soups.

Egg noodles

For example, Chinese hokkien and Indonesian bami. Like Western egg noodles, they're made from wheat flour and egg. May be round, ranging from thin to thick (ideal for wok stir-frying) as well as flat and thin for soups and braised dishes—usually prepared by boiling. Wonton skins are square or round egg-noodle sheets that can be used for dumplings in soup or steamed or fried for dim sum. You'll find wonton skins in the refrigerated section of an Asian market.

Cellophane (mung bean thread) noodles (photo left)

Long, thin, transparent noodles made from the starch of mung beans, sweet potatoes, potatoes, arrowroot, etc. For soups and salads. Soaked in water and sometimes also boiled briefly.

Rice noodles (photo right)

Made from rice and water. Mainly found in Southeast Asia, ranging from angel hair-thin to papardelle-thick. Depending on the type, they're used for soups, salads, braised dishes and wok stir-fries—they can be boiled briefly or soaked in hot water before using.

Wheat noodles

For example, somen (spaghetti-thin for cold dishes and soups), udon (thicker) and ramen (medium-thick for soups), all of which are Japanese. Like Italian pasta, they're made from wheat flour and water—and prepared by parboiling. Chinese mi, mie or mee noodles are often classified as wheat noodles but are actually pasta that was shaped into blocks before drying. Those are best cooked according to the package directions.

Noodles
Asian Style

More creative than rice.
More fun than pasta.

When rice appears on an Asian table, it's usually as a soloist, accompanied by an orchestra of clinking platters filled with various delicacies. When noodles are served, the meal turns into a jam session of sizzling woks and bubbling soup pots. Asian noodles are straight out of everyday life and always bring something extra to your bowl, whether in a Peking-style soup or in an Indonesian goreng.

In Asia, noodles symbolize a long life, especially if the noodles themselves are long. In the Far East, variety is achieved through content rather than form. Wheat, buckwheat, rice and legumes provide the flour and starch from which Asian noodles are made. Although the noodles are generally cooked only briefly, they're sometimes even extra slippery—perfect for slurping. And since they aren't immediately mixed in with the sauce when served, Asian noodles are usually rinsed under cold water after draining. This keeps them from sticking together if they're added to a wok or soup later on (after being dipped briefly in hot water).

Boiling Noodles

For most wheat, egg and rice noodles and some cellophane noodles: Bring 1 quart unsalted water (though you can salt the water if you like) to a boil per 3 1/2 oz. noodles and cook noodles no longer than the time indicated on the package. To be safe, test periodically toward the end of the cooking time.

Parboiling Noodles

For soba, somen and udon: Bring 1 quart unsalted water to a boil per 3 1/2 ounces noodles. Once the water boils, add a 1/4 cup water to halt the boiling. Bring to a boil once again and once again add cold water. Keep this up until the noodles are done (two to four times). Drain and rinse under cold water.

Soaking Noodles

For very thin rice noodles and most cellophane noodles, you simply need to soak them by pouring hot to boiling water over the top. Occasionally you'll also have to bring them to a boil briefly (experiment and see what fits your taste). In any case, rinse these noodles under cold water before using.

Vegetables & Herbs Asian Style

These are what make the markets so green and the cuisine so fresh.

Asian cuisine can be as picturesque and fresh as a farmer's wife harvesting her Chinese long beans three times a year, a farmer transporting a wagonload of spinach to the next village, a market vendor displaying his or her vegetables in a beautiful spread or a wife going to the market before preparing each meal. These scenes in the United States can be rare, though they do exist. Those who live in large cities might have access to Asian markets filled with fresh greens for exotic dishes; others may have a local farmer's market. The rest of us have to make do with whatever we can find at typical supermarkets or produce markets. Is that bad?

Not as bad as you'd think. As we've already said, freshness is the most important ingredient in Asian cooking. Since many of our standard vegetables are also found in Asian cuisine, no matter where you live you should be able to cook it. Even if you're in the country! Chances are, you can buy dew-covered Swiss chard from the farmer next door to stir-fry in your wok instead of imported bok choy from a Chinese market.

For the recipes in Basic Asian, we based our choice of vegetables on this principle of freshness. First, under the heading "Found Everywhere," we list vegetables such as green onions that are used in both Asian and Western cuisines. Then under "Found in Asian Markets" are vegetables that are often imported. Finally, "Try It Out" lists uncommon vegetables popular in Asia—ones you might stumble across in an Asian market—and you may just have to try them!

Leafy Vegetables

Asia's favorite vegetables, these colorful greens brighten up the markets.

Found Everywhere
Chinese (napa) cabbage: For salads and wok stir-frying.
White/green cabbage: For salads, pickling, soups and wok stir-frying.

Found in Asian Markets
Banana leaves: From the banana palm, for garnishing and for wrapping food during cooking (e.g., fish). Substitute: Aluminum foil or parchment.
Bok Choy (photo above): Fast-cooking mustard cabbage that is Asia's universal vegetable. Ideal for the wok, in stews and for braising. Substitute: Chinese cabbage, Swiss chard and even romaine.

Try It Out
Choy sum: Extremely tender leafy cabbage, ideal for the same uses as bok choy.
Gai lan: Chinese broccoli with delicious stems and leaves—fantastic in the wok.

Root Vegetables

As the earthy counterpart to the tender leaves above; they give dishes substance.

Found Everywhere
Carrots: For everything from a raw snack to curries that are stewed for hours.
Radishes with greens: For salads, dips and wok stir-frying.
Turnips: For wok stir-frying, stews and braised dishes.

Found in Asian Markets
Sweet Potatoes: Mainly used in India; starchy tubers used for curries, braising and deep-frying. Substitute: Starchy potatoes.

Try It Out
Daikon: Asian radish with a mild flavor. For pickling and braising.

Colorful Vegetables

These serve to enrich Asian cuisine.

Found Everywhere
Bell peppers: For wok stir-frying, braising, sautéing and pickling.
Broccoli: For wok stir-frying and braising.
Cauliflower: For wok stir-frying and braising.
Celery: For wok stir-frying, braising, soups, salads and snacks.
Cucumbers: For salads, dips, pickling and braising. Asian cucumbers are shorter and more aromatic than Western varieties with more seeds and tougher peels.
Eggplant: For wok stir-frying, braising, grilling, deep-frying and stuffing. Shapes, colors and sizes vary.
Green asparagus: Cut in half lengthwise, or sliced at an angle into sections, it's great for wok stir-frying, sautéing and braising.
Green beans: For stews, braising, sautéing, wok stir-frying and salads.
Green onions: Together with garlic and ginger,

they make up the trio used to prepare many wok dishes, soups, sautéed and braised dishes.

Leek: The green onion's larger sibling used in the same way, plus as a vegetable side dish.

Pumpkin: For soups, stews, braising, deep-frying, grilling and pickling.

Found in Asian Markets

Asian cucumbers and eggplant: See above under cucumbers and eggplant.

Green papaya: Firm, unripe fruit grated for salads and dips or cut into very fine strips—often mixed with fish sauce.

Try It Out

Chinese long beans: Thin and up to 3 feet long. They can be cut up and used just like beans. But remember, they cook quicker and also tend to spoil quickly.

Sprouts & Legumes

Highly esteemed in India; we can find them in health-food stores and Turkish markets.

Found Everywhere

Bean sprouts: What we know of as soybean sprouts are often the seedlings of green mung beans. For stir-frying, salads and as a condiment.

Red lentils: Indian "masoor dal." Dried, used for soups, curries, salads and as a side dish.

Snow peas: For wok stir-frying, salads and soups.

Found in Asian Markets

Bamboo shoots: They're harvested before sprouting; typically found in cans. For stir-frying, salads, braising and soups.

Chickpeas: Indian "kala chana." Dried, used for soups and braising.

True soybean sprouts: Longer than mung bean sprouts. Often blanched.

Try It Out

Black mung beans: Indian "sabat urid." Usually shelled and then called "urid dal." For stews, braising and side dishes.

Dried mung beans: Usually shelled as Indian "moong dal." For soups, salads and rice dishes.

Mushrooms

Found Everywhere

Oyster mushrooms: Originally from Asia. These cook quickly and have a slightly meaty flavor. For wok stir-frying, salads and braising.

Shiitake mushrooms: Originally from Japan. More aromatic than white mushrooms; the tough stems must be removed. They have a more intense flavor when dried. For wok stir-frying, soups, braising, salads and grilling.

Found in Asian Markets

Dried mushrooms: For example, shiitake. For wok stir-frying, soups and braising—they must be soaked in hot water prior to use.

Herbs & Seasonings

Found Everywhere

Chile peppers, cilantro, ginger: Found in more and more stores and markets. Want more info? See pages 12–15.

Mint: Common mint will work in Asian dishes, but Vietnamese mint is best.

Found in Asian Markets

Asian mint: The kind of mint they like in Thailand, Vietnam and India. "Vietnamese mint" is the name to look for.

Galangal, kaffir lime leaves, lemon grass: Read about these on pages 12–15.

Thai basil: Tastes more minty and peppery than sweet basil and closer to anise than to cloves—fantastic in Southeast Asian dishes. You can substitute sweet basil.

Try It out

Asian chives: These taste like leek and garlic—but, again, it's fine to use standard chives. Good for wok stir-frying and for cooking with fish and eggs.

Curry leaves: Not contained in curry powder or paste but they give curries unique flavor.

Soy
Asian Style

You say it has no flavor?

"The cheese of Asia, the perfect food, the food of the future. In a word, Tofu." Wait a minute, are we talking about the same thing? Those white blocks waiting around in health-food stores and Asian markets for someone to take them home so they can then retort, "Na, na, fooled you! I'm nothing and I taste like nothing!"

Actually, tofu has a lot to offer. Just think of it in terms of a grilled cheese sandwich. The reason a cheese sandwich tastes good is because of the cheese, but the cheese doesn't taste nearly as good without buttered, toasted bread. It's the same with tofu—it's not the cheese that brings out the full aroma, it's the bread and butter. Take, for instance, silken tofu, which soaks up all the fine flavor of miso soup into itself. Speaking of which, if you combine tofu with soy sauce and other intense seasonings, it soaks up all those flavors as well. In that sense, it always takes on the taste of its surroundings.

Other proofs of the versatility and depth of this inconspicuous substance are all the things soy can be turned into: milk, flour, oil, miso, sauce, mayonnaise, bean sprouts, smoked foods, breakfast cereals, bean stews and chocolate. Not all of these are especially Asian but are good nonetheless.

How Tofu is Made

Dried soybeans are soaked, ground with water and squeezed out. The milk thus produced is brought to a boil and gypsum (scientific name: calcium sulphate) or a sea-salt extract is added to cause it to curdle. This mixture is then poured into small baskets lined with cloth that are drained and gently pressed into tofu blocks.

Buying Tofu

The heat-sealed tofu packages in the refrigerated section of the Asian market may be convenient but what you gain in authenticity you lose in freshness and sacrifice to extra additives. That's why it's better to choose the fresher tofu made locally and stored in water-filled tubs. This assumes that the seller changes the water daily and replaces all merchandise every one to two days. Once you get it home, you need to change the tofu water daily and use up the whole block within five days. Or, purchase tofu in individual water-packed containers. Health food stores are another great place to check for quality tofu.

Tofu & Soy Basics

Miso paste
See pages 12–15.

Silken tofu
Soft tofu with the consistency of firm custard. A coagulant is added to cold soy milk. This milk is then transferred to containers in which it is heated and then sets. Good for soups, salads, braising and dessert. Can also be steamed, deep-fried, stir-fried, sautéed and stewed. Works for miso soup.

Soy milk
Pressed out of soybeans that have been ground with water and boiled. A base for drinks, desserts and Asian and Western soy milk products (e.g., soy yogurt). Also an ideal liquid for stewing.

Soy sauce
See pages 12–15.

Special varieties
These types of tofu are very firm and dry, prepared like regular tofu (often with salt or other flavors), pressed for a longer period of time and sometimes cooked in a spiced liquid. It's also seasoned and used for cold dishes and snacks, and unseasoned for sautéing, stir-frying and braising. It may be smoked, deep-fried or pickled.

Tempeh
Indonesian whole-grain, fermented tofu with a nutty flavor. Soybeans are soaked, de-hulled, split in half and boiled. A fermenting agent is then added and the mixture is wrapped in leaves, plastic film or foil. The finished "tempeh sausages" are sliced and marinated, deep-fried, sautéed or braised.

Tofu (photo left)
In Basic Asian, this refers to the relatively firm "semi-soft tofu" that has a consistency ranging from that of soft feta to firm mozzarella, depending on how it's pressed. Sometimes precooked, it's good for pickling, wokking, sautéing, grilling, deep-frying, braising and baking. There's also fried tofu, which has a golden skin on it.

Fruit
Asian Style

For those of you who still expect dessert in Chinese restaurants

Those who pass their lives under the palms in Southeast Asia have a sweeter take on Asian cuisine than the people in the northern Asia. That's because they have all the tropical fruit they could possibly want, for eating both raw and cooked. And since Asia's exotic fruits taste so out of this world—different from Western fruits—they've managed to distribute their fruits to even the smallest-town stores in the United States.

Some of the fruits, like lemons, have settled in with us as long-time residents; others, like bananas, as naturalized citizens; still others, like mangos, as familiar friends; and some, like fresh lychees, as appealing strangers we'd like to get to know better. And all it takes to enjoy them is a few tricks of the hand with a knife, maybe a dash of lemon or lime and they're ready to eat! Beyond that, even Asian cooks do nothing more than use them for salads, deep-fried dishes or drinks. They want no part of all the egg-breaking and flour-kneading we put ourselves through to make dessert. At the same time, many spicy Asian dishes are incomplete without the sweet and sour flavor of fruit, or of their peel and leaves—such as those of the kaffir lime.

Storing Exotic Fruits

Two or three temperatures are involved. First there's the ripening temperature ranging from 53 to 77°F, the temperature at which exotic fruits grow in their native habitat and at which they're ripened in storage once harvested. Then there's the storage temperature from 32 to 57°F that slows down the ripening process while the fruit is being transported—also the ideal temperature for keeping most ripe exotic fruits fresh.

Since sensitive tropical fruits are harvested before they ripen (except for fruits that can't be ripened in storage, such as lychees) and are then kept in cold storage, you often have to ripen them at home. Depending on the fruit, the ideal location is either a cool cellar or a warm living room. Many fruits give off the gas ethylene while ripening, which causes sensitive fruit to ripen faster but also to spoil faster. These gas producers include bananas, mangos, nashi, papaya, passion fruit and rambutan as well as apples, apricots, pears, peaches and nectarines. Fruits that are sensitive to this gas (meaning, don't ripen them alongside the gas-producing types) include persimmon, kiwi and mangosteen along with cherries, melons and plums.

But Now Let's
Wok!

It's one thing to take a stroll through the market and learn about all the wonderful ingredients available. But making something out of them is quite another. Cooking the ingredients means work because you have to chop, stir-fry and do it all just right. So where's the yin and yang?

Even the leftover rice you just finished stir- frying contains something of its gentle sources of the day before that harbor the legacy of the ancestors' advice: "Take heed, my child, never fry freshly cooked rice!" Inside the half-sphere of the wok, all these elements unite with the good things in your kitchen to restore you to fullness, happiness and health.

What's the recipe for this? Your inner Chinese chef will tell you: "Recipes are only words—don't put all your trust in them." Instead, take what you've learned about the ingredients and ask yourself more important questions such as, "Who's coming to dinner? What do I have in the refrigerator? What should I make in the wok now?" On the next few pages, we offer a few suggestions regarding the most important methods of Asian cooking preparation. But the rest is up to you. Just make something. Preferably, the best you can and preferably right away!

Wok Stir-Frying

This means stirring up a lot of little things over fairly high heat for a relatively short period of time until you have something truly delicious.

Starter Kit

So, let's get started—with the wok, of course. It's important your wok be large and able to withstand high heat. The best are the thin-walled iron woks with a rounded base set over a high gas flame—but a flat-bottomed wok on a large electric burner also works. You can also use a large frying pan. A nice touch is a handle you can use to shake the wok while your stir. Then you just need a wok spatula (or a wooden spoon if that's all you have) or long cooking chopsticks for stirring.

What to Stir-Fry

Since wok stir-frying is a "Formula 1" cooking method, only the fully prepared are allowed at the starting line. This means everything has to be cut up correctly and placed, ready and waiting, into small bowls before cooking. Cut each vegetable or chunk of meat into uniform pieces for cooking efficiently and quickly over high heat. More tender ingredients must be chopped larger and firmer must be chopped smaller. Sometimes ingredients are also precooked or marinated, after which they must be patted dry.

Wokking Right

Heat up the wok, add oil, heat it and then swirl it around; pour it out into another heat-proof container. Now heat 1–2 tablespoons more oil. If you're stir-frying noodles, rice, meat, fish or seafood, add them first, stir fry briefly until lightly golden, and then remove them. Otherwise add the base flavorings (e.g., garlic, green onions, ginger, chile peppers, lemon grass and the like) and stir constantly. Next add vegetables, progressing from the firmer to the more tender—and stir, stir, stir. Finally, pour in your cooking liquid (stock, rice wine, etc.) and then you can briefly re-heat the pre-cooked ingredients such as rice noodles and meat. Then add chopped herbs if desired. That's all there is to it! If you really want to be fancy you can fry each ingredient separately, then combine them all together with the liquid.

Steaming

Steaming renders food calm and tranquil, like subdued lighting or hushed music. Just think about shrimp steamed with ginger and rice. Suddenly, life is more peaceful.

Starter Kit

The nice thing about Asian bamboo steamers is that they're authentic, they've been working just fine for centuries, they're nice to look at, they're inexpensive and they come in different sizes. This makes them the first choice for steaming. To use, put a little water in a wok or large frying pan and set the steamer inside so it rests securely in the pan and the liquid is under the steamer. Or you can steam in deep pot: sit a plate on top of an upside-down cup; add liquid to the bottom of the pan and steam foods on the plate, with the pan covered. Or use a steamer insert inside a covered pot.

What to Steam and How

Because of their tenderness, fish, seafood and light poultry are ideal for steaming. Although this process takes longer than boiling (a method rarely used in Asian cuisine), it brings out the full aroma. This is especially true when a marinade is used, which can also be used as part of the steaming liquid. The pieces should be of uniform size and not too small so every-thing will stay juicy. Something large like a whole fish should be scored for the same reason. A steamer is also used for cooking dim sum wrapped in noodle dough or rice paper.

Steaming Right

To keep the food from sticking to the bamboo basket, you must line it while making sure enough steam can still get through. Traditional liners include Chinese cabbage and parchment paper. You can also use spinach, lettuce or cucumber slices, and using onion rings and herb bouquets will add extra flavor. Place the food to be cooked on top and, if desired, drizzle it with seasoning sauce or marinade. If you want the food to steam in its own juices, place food in a dish resting on the steamer basket. Fill a wok about a third full of water or a pot until the water reaches halfway up the sides of the upside-down cup (mentioned above). The water should not boil vigorously. When the water boils, insert the

basket (filled with food) and cover with the lid (real pros stack several baskets on top of one another, covered). Now just wait for the amount of time stated in the recipe and please don't raise the lid to peek or the steam will escape! When the food is done, you can also season it with various herbs or other flavorings.

Deep-Frying

Asian chefs can't understand why some of their sophisticated Western colleagues are so proud of not using deep-frying as a cooking technique. They also don't feel the need for deep-frying machines. To them, the wok does double duty for creating delicious deep-fried dishes.

Starter Kit

Once again the kit includes a wok because woks are ideal for deep-frying. Because of its curved base, a wok offers a lot of room for frying while using less oil, its temperature is easy to regulate quickly and it's easier to clean than a deep-fryer. A large slotted metal utensil will help you remove everything from the oil. A wire rack that fits around the inside edge of the wok is convenient for draining cooked ingredients and also for keeping them warm.

What to Deep-Fry and How

Cooked noodles (patted dry) and potatoes can be deep-fried without a coating because their starch binds with moisture and prevents them from shrinking. Shrimp and fish or vegetables cut into bite-size chunks should be coated with a liquid batter to protect them from the hot oil. Small and delicate pieces of fish or vegetables can be wrapped in a firmer dough—as in the case of spring rolls. Most importantly, pieces of meat should be pre-cooked so deep-frying will leave them crispy on the outside and cooked through and juicy on the inside.

Deep-Frying Right

Fill the wok no more than a third full of high-heat, neutral tasting cooking oil such as canola or peanut oil and heat it to 350°F. How do you know when it's this hot? Hold the handle of a wooden spoon in the oil. When a lot of tiny bubbles dance around the handle, you can start frying. Now add just enough pieces (either plain or dipped in batter) so they all have room without cooling off the oil too much. Deep-fry it all for 1–2 minutes until crispy while still light, just the way Asian chefs do. This is why Asians also like to fry spring rolls twice, first at only about 325°F (if necessary, measure temperature with a cooking thermometer) so they're nice and light and again at 350°F to give them a crispy light finish. The wok even allows you to deep-fry whole fish. Score the fish two or three times on the side and then place it in the hot oil so it covers it. This will leave it both crispy and juicy. In Asia they also love to aromatize the oil briefly beforehand with garlic, ginger or chile peppers.

Braising and more

Limiting the Asian culinary arts to wok stir-frying, steaming and deep-frying would be like making a painting with only blue, yellow and green. It might be good but after a while it feels like something is missing. Like braising, simmering, marinating, grilling and roasting.

Marinating

In Asia this not only refers to seasoning by soaking but also to making the best of an ingredient by changing its flavor and structure. Sometimes it may be the only "cooking" method used, as in cabbage pickled for Korean kimchi. Or sometimes it's a step that leads up to the final dish, as in the case of marinated, oven-roasted pork.

Grilling & Roasting

A cold or room-temperature marinade often leads up to these fiery hot cooking methods in which the seasoning is forced into the interior of the cooked food with concentrated cooking power. This is the case with Japan's yakitori skewers that are diligently brushed with marinade as they lie above the hot coals, or Peking duck whose air-dried honey marinade gives it a sheen and aroma in the hot oven air.

Braising

This is where Asian cuisine starts to resemble European methods of stewing in a sauce and pot-roasting—but with an artistry all its own, of course. In this case, fattier meats such as pork and duck or rich fish are braised in a mixture of rice wine, soy sauce, sugar and spices such as anise, cinnamon and coriander. This liquid is reduced to a thick, reddish sauce that penetrates into the meat. To achieve the highest level of perfection, you can also deep-fry the pieces afterwards.

Simmering

This is an extremely gentle method of poaching. Chicken (and, sometimes, pork) is first gently simmered in water, then removed from the heat and left to itself. Next, it is plunged into ice water and then refrigerated overnight, turning it into the perfect chicken—snow-white meat tender as butter with the juice jelled under a silky firm skin, excellent in soups and salads. Also see the method for chicken cooked in Master Stock (page 127).

17 handy items
for Asian Style cuisine

Wok

The wok base, separate from the wok, stabilizes the round-bottom wok on the burner, with its concave bottom curving downward inside the ring over a gas flame. This centers the heat precisely at the curve in the wok to which the ingredients always slide during stir-frying. Thin-walled Asian iron woks are ideal. Like cast-iron woks, they are cleaned with water alone and then oiled. Western flat-bottomed woks are a good alternative and are used without a base on either gas or electric cooktops. Non-stick woks, on the other hand, wear out quickly when exposed to high heat, and so are not ideal.

Bamboo Steamer

If a wok were built like a bamboo steamer, it would be as pretty as a rice farmer's hat but would have a shorter life span. Not so in the case of the bamboo steamer because it always has water and the wok to stand between it and the flames. We find this steamer better than the popular stainless steel version and happen to believe that fish tastes better steamed in bamboo than in metal. A diameter of 8 to 10 inches makes an adequate standard model; the smaller ones are for dim sum only. After use, rinse it with plain water (no soap) and then dry it well so it won't get moldy.

Knives

Cleavers are a great addition to your Western blade collection. Use a narrow one for fine cutting, a heavy one for chopping, or a medium one for both—to start out. The cleaver blade is often made of plain steel, which is sharp, but also susceptible to rust. You can prevent this by drying and oiling it well. The same applies to Japanese knives whose blades comprise a soft layer surrounding a hard core and are sharpened on one side. But be careful with these because they're razor-sharp and can quickly spoil you when you're used to using your old knives.

Sushi Mat

Even if the "makisu" represents only one country (Japan) and is used to make a single dish (maki sushi), the recipe for which isn't even included in this book (but can be found in *Basic Cooking*), the bamboo mat is still one of the most widespread Asian cooking implements in the world, after the wok. It can be as large as a placemat with round or semicircular slats. And thanks to its flexibility, it makes it very easy for a trained person to roll sushi rice in nori sheets. Afterwards the mat is scrubbed with plain water and dried well so the next maki sushi will taste only of maki sushi.

Mortar & Pestle

This is the peppermill of Asia except that besides those spicy grains, it can also be used to grind almost every other spice in the world. After all, most of these spices grow in the Far Southeast, which is why the people there don't think much of commercially-ground spices. They would rather roast cinnamon sticks, anise stars, coriander or cumin seeds, cool them, throw them into a mortar and grind or crush them finely with a matching, rounded pestle. If they add a fresh ingredient, such as an herb, they make a paste. But the one thing that can't go in a mortar is soap—otherwise your next curry will leave you disappointed.

Fortune Cookie

Have you ever gotten a bad fortune from a fortune cookie? These sugary wafers contain the best of positive thinking, which is no surprise when you consider their origin. They were invented in the early 20th century by an Asian restaurant owner in sunny California whose American guests wanted dessert and he had none to give. There's some confusion about the original (Japanese rice cracker or Chinese moon cake?) and the inventor (proprietor of a Chinese noodle house or a Japanese teahouse?). Maybe no one has ever sought an answer except on the inside of a fortune cookie.

Spatula

If you want to stir-fry correctly, you need a wok spatula. The Western variety is usually wooden while the Asian is more often metal with a rounded edge so it can seamlessly follow the curve of the wok. Cooking chopsticks, which are more than twice as long as ordinary chopsticks and are sometimes joined at the end, are also used for stirring and in the place of tongs, for turning individual pieces while deep-frying. Otherwise, for removing foods from deep-frying oil, use a large slotted metal utensil.

Condiment Servers

This is as much a part of modest Asian restaurants as laminate tables and the constant sizzling of a wok. The condiment servers contains the little hot and spicy sides and sauces in bottles, glasses, jars and boxes, ready for you to help yourself. Fiery sambals and dried whole chiles or chile flakes are just waiting for bowls of noodle soup; fresh cilantro adds its heavenly scent and thick oyster sauce gently glug-glugs out of the bottle to complement the rice just fried. Here's an idea—set out these holders at your next Asian party at home!

Chopsticks

The first time you try to eat with chopsticks might also be the first time you realize that what's natural to you—eating with a knife and fork—is anything but natural to a large part of humanity. Chinese eat almost everything with flat-sided chopsticks and Japanese with rounded ones, whereas Southeast Asians prefer using a spoon and their fingers. There are also rules of etiquette for chopsticks, such as never lick your chopsticks, never stick them straight down into rice, never point them at anyone and always lay them down on the chopstick rest or on their paper wrapper.

Hot Towels

It's so easy to feel like a maharaja or at least a first-class passenger on an Asian airline. Just roll up a couple small terrycloth towels, heat and moisten them in the bamboo steamer and then wipe your hands, forehead and neck with them—and life just became more serene. In Asia, this small and very effective ritual before a meal serves to wash off the dust of everyday life and free you for the delights to come. After a meal, it signals your return to the outside world, strengthened and ready for the next dust cloud. Wouldn't that be something nice to offer your guests?

Board

This is another item from Asian cuisine that still looks the same as it did thousands of years ago. That's because it was already perfect. Asian cutting boards are round because they were originally cross sections of logs. The ideal has a diameter of about one foot, is 2 to 4 inches thick and is made of hardwood. If you scrub it thoroughly after use and oil it once in a while, it will remain in good shape. A square wooden board also works. Plastic might not get along with the sharp cleaver. And should your cutting board have little feet like the one in our photo? It can but doesn't have to.

Cushions

Whether as part of a tea ceremony in a Japanese pavilion, in the back room of a Cantonese teahouse or under the roof of an Indian dining tent, eating on the floor—or rather, sitting on the floor while you eat—is typically Asian. Traditionally, men sit cross-legged and women with both legs off to one side, their knees bent. At home, all you need is a bunch of cushions around a coffee table to create this exotic feeling while you enjoy your steaming rice and fragrant spices.

Bowls

The Chinese not only invented porcelain but also gave it the ideal shape. The roundness of the bowl exactly fits your hand as you slurp your soup. It's also easy to hold in your hand at chest-height, the better to eat your rice and braised meat with chopsticks. Other ideal items made of porcelain or earthenware include large bowls for side dishes and sauces, platters and plates for banquet-style foods, and won ton soup spoons.

17 handy items for Asian Style cuisine

Teapot

In China, the four prerequisites for enjoying tea are fine tea, good water, beautiful surroundings and a complete tea service. These serve to create a feeling of harmony. This may take the form of a magical infusion in a clay pot, or an equally pleasurable brew in a white porcelain pot decorated with a rice-grain pattern. Japan has teapots of enameled cast iron, India likes them silver-plated and in everyday life in Asia, the pot is often just a cup with a lid on top and tea leaves inside to which water is repeatedly added.

Cups

The typical Asian drinking vessels are the small, simply or elaborately decorated porcelain cups for drinking rice wine that are often accompanied by an equally small carafe. Guests never fill their own cups from the carafe but only those of their fellow drinkers with the silent understanding that the others will do the same for them. This applies equally to all other drinks in the Far East, which are served in glasses just as they are in the West. But we almost forgot to mention Japan where in some regions sake is consumed at the start of a meal from small cedar boxes, the rims of which are sprinkled with salt.

Lantern

Just hanging something colorful and billowy from the ceiling can immediately make a room feel a little Asian, whether it's a lantern for the spring festival, a dragon for the moon festival or a windsock disguised as a Japanese carp. Red and gold folding lampshades available in Asian stores, though kitschy, can add atmosphere. Hang them over your ceiling light and your dining table becomes the Shanghai Bar Chinoise. But if you'd rather evoke the tropical Southeast, we suggest you suspend a hammock between potted palms for decoration.

Buddha

What part does Buddha play in Asian cuisine? A big one if you consider the statues of this frequently smiling deity as he's portrayed in China in all his grand corpulence. However, there's also the well-built youth and athlete as he appears in Southeast Asian figures. Basically, we use him here as the symbol of a cuisine that is so tightly bound to philosophy, religion, medicine, nature and humanity that it doesn't have to conform to headlines or fashion. Every day it adapts to life just as life adapts to it. You'll find more about this on the next page.

Balance

How everything comes together and is finally perfected, why the final step is always followed by another first, and what tightrope walking can teach us about Asian cooking. It all comes down to yin and yang.

Tightrope walking is basically simple. The path lies clearly before you in a straight line. You can see that this path is the only way to the goal and that any step to the side will take you away from it. There are no forks in the road and no choices. And yet every journey from one end of the rope to the other is an adventure for the acrobat. It makes no difference how well they're trained or how much they know about gravity. The rope sways differently every time and the walker must adapt to it. The same is true of Asian-style cooking. In theory, it's simple but in practice, it's an adventure. Knowledge and practice will help you master it but in the end, it's your attitude that determines whether you'll achieve balance—the highest goal of Asian cuisine.

In fact, very few Asian chefs or home cooks have memorized all the ayurvedic styles or the yins and yangs by which they're supposed to cook. But they still do it well and correctly because it's in their blood, thanks to a centuries-old tradition of cooking and eating that continues to be integral to their lives to the present day. Let's follow their lead and seek wisdom closer to home—in the kitchen. Starting now.

The Props

For trapeze artists, it's a tightrope and a pole; for cooks, it's the ingredients. The ingredients determine how balance will finally be achieved. It isn't so much about presenting a particular ingredient to its best possible advantage. In Asia, a particular food is good only if it makes its own contribution to the success of the meal as a whole. That's why conscientious Asian chefs would rather not cook at all than use ingredients that are not fresh or are out of season. They'd rather try to change the recipe and achieve the balance with a substitution.

The Forces

For trapeze artists, these are the steps they take on the tightrope; for cooks the forces are their methods of preparation. These affect the props and create the forward motion to get things going. Whether a piece of fish is wok stir-fried, steamed or marinated while raw determines its contribution to the dish as a whole, meaning it directs the course of the cooking process. Thus, it directs how the other ingredients will be handled.

Balance

Now it's a matter of harmonizing the props and the forces. Asian chefs have mastered this art to perfection. They know how to extract everything an ingredient has to offer plus throw in one or two surprises. They understand how to apply various methods of preparation to a single dish and they know how to combine it all successfully.

Reaching the Goal

For trapeze artists, the goal is the end of the rope; for cooks it's the dinner table, the center of Asian life. This is a place of meeting, exchange and relaxation, as well as eating, where even the most successful dish is only part of a whole. A dish really isn't complete until it has contributed to making the gathering special. So if you've been getting more and more anxious as you've been reading, you can relax now. If plain, grilled skewers among friends bring more joy than high-stress, complicated sushi, then they're exactly the right dish for your meal.

Curiosity

So now you've created a perfect dish, simple but sensational. Will you ever manage to do it again? Could you do it even better? Would a different ingredient make it even more delicious? As you can see, even perfection is only a part of a whole and the final step is always followed by another first. Yin and yang, in other words. Excuse me? What is that? Could you explain that a little more clearly?

Yin and Yang

For Chinese philosophers, the culinary arts were a realm for putting their theories into practice. Confucius dealt in the culture of cooking, including the marriage of flavor, aroma, structure and appearance within a meal. Lao Tse preached the doctrine of yin and yang, the credo of which is $1 + 1 = 3$. In other words, the feminine, soft, cool, tranquil, expanding "yin" plus the masculine, hard, warm, active, contracting "yang" results in a joint yin and yang experience. Too complicated? Okay, every object contains some yin and some yang and every object is shaped by the relationship between the two and how they are handled. Delicate fish, for example, has a little more yin than yang. When you add soy sauce (salty and very yin) it becomes even more yin. Rice wine (extremely yang) balances this out. Delicate fish is balanced harmoniously when served in a soy and rice wine sauce.

Very yin: Alcohol, sugar, vinegar, beverages, tropical fruits, spices.
Yin: Most vegetables, seaweed, delicate fish, some seafood, nuts, tofu.
Neutral: Grains.
Yang: Rich fish, some seafood, light meat, poultry, eggs, vegetables cooked for a long time, sake.
Very yang: Salty, dark meat.

the recipes

Start

"Should we start eating?" Yes, of course!

ers

Starting can be a big production at Asian meals. For instance, in China, it takes time for all the diners to enter the door in the correct customary order and find their places at the large round table.

But then in Southeast Asia things are so casual that the question, "Should we start eating?" rarely causes any movement at all. And then, all of a sudden, all the dishes appear on the table—all at once. In fact, many times Asian meals are not served in courses but with everything served at one time.

In the United States, we place a few starters on the table as a signal. Though the dishes in this section may, in Asia, be thought of as snacks, street food, or sides served along with a large meal, we bring them into our culture as appetizers. And there's nothing wrong with that...what better than some Vietnamese spring rolls or Indian pakoras to get things going? Let's start eating!

Finger Exercise No. 1
Eating with Chopsticks

As you master this exercise, you will feel a growing tranquility whenever you're confronted with a bowl of rice... especially in an Asian restaurant when all your friends are using chopsticks!

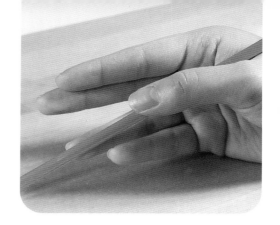

1. Grasp the first chopstick firmly in the crease of your thumb with the end resting on the tip of your ring finger. Use your pinky to stabilize it if necessary. From now on, it shouldn't move.

2. Hold the second chopstick parallel to the first with a small gap between the two and hold it between the tips of your thumb, index, and middle fingers. From now on, it should remain mobile.

3. Now lift the rice bowl toward your mouth and try out your newfound skill. Use your index and middle finger to open the "tongs" and when you successfully nab some rice, try to bring it up to your mouth without dropping any. When you can manage a mouthful of rice, you earn the orange belt; when you can lift a single grain, you graduate to black belt.

Dear Aunt Betty,

It seems like we just finished celebrating my departure with your famous volcano cake and here I am in the Hong Kong Hotel. First thing this morning I told the cab driver at the airport that I wanted a "real Chinese breakfast." He took me to a gigantic teahouse where the hosts navigate among the large, round tables communicating by way of walkie talkies. Since all the big families in Hong Kong were taking up most of the space, I ended up at a tiny table by the kitchen door watching endless carts of steamer baskets going in and out. Whenever one of the cart-pushers said something to me, I nodded. So within 5 minutes, I had 23 baskets full of dumplings and chicken feet in front of me. A group of New Zealanders came to my rescue. They invited me to their table and held the waitresses at bay until we'd finished off the last claw, when the whole thing started up again. As Confucius says, "The solitary person is an emperor at dawn and emperors don't belong in dim sum restaurants."

With that in mind,

Your niece, Louise

12.06.2002
POST
Basic Services
5

To:
Aunt Betty
123 Homesick Lane
Des Moines, Iowa
United States

Homemade Asian Basics
Sushi Ginger

Everything has its yin and yang. That's why fresh sushi needs to be balanced by the freshest of sushi ginger. But often the exact taste left behind by the readymade pickled ginger served in sushi bars unpleasantly resembles cleaning solution. So what do you do if you don't want to treat your tongue like a sink? Obviously, you make your own very fresh pickled ginger:

Peel $2/3$ pound of ginger and slice very finely with a mandoline or with a vegetable peeler. Then boil it in water for about 30 seconds, drain and place in a bowl. Heat $1\frac{1}{4}$ cups sake, 3 teaspoons sugar (or $1\frac{1}{4}$ cups mirin and 1 teaspoon sugar), and 2 teaspoons salt and pour over sliced ginger. Marinate for at least 24 hours.

Or a more modern version: Peel $2/3$ pound of ginger and slice truly paper-thin using a mandoline or vegetable peeler. Boil briefly as described above. Bring to a boil 1 $\frac{1}{4}$ cups rice vinegar, 2 tablespoons fish sauce, and 1 table-spoon sugar. Pour over the ginger along with $1/3$ cup fresh-squeezed lime juice and marinate for 2 days.

Both will keep in the refrigerator for a week and make enough for 20–30 hungry sushi guests. For a smaller quantity of pickled ginger, feel free to halve either of the recipes.

Drinking Asian Style:
Tea

Tea is to Asia what wine is to southern Europe: They drink it because it's there and because it's always been there. The fact that tea drinking is healthy, wise and therefore pretty trendy is old news to the Chinese. The same way that French are versed in wine, Asians are knowledgeable about tea. What amounts to a cult outside Asia is, inside Asia, simply a part of everyday life.

Just as you have white, red and rosé wines, you also have green tea from dried leaves, black tea from previously fermented leaves and oolong tea from only slightly fermented leaves. And just as Europe is divided into wine territories or appellations, Asia can roughly be divided into black tea regions in the North and West and green tea regions in the South and East. Wine's late harvest is tea's first flush. Is tea really just the next generation's wine?

Not likely! Whereas grapes really become interesting only after the harvest, that's when tea leaves are most mundane. What about vintage, cultivation, aging, you say? Never mind would be the answer of most Asians. Just open the bag, pour hot water over it and it's done. Let's follow their lead and drink tea just because it's there. Let's make sure we always have some on hand—and when we no longer need to remind ourselves that each swallow makes us wiser, we will have achieved true wisdom.

Making tea: Bring $2\frac{1}{2}$ cups cold water to a boil. Swirl hot tap water around in the teapot and pour it out. Place 2-3 teaspoons loose green or black tea leaves in a wide strainer lowered into the teapot. For black tea, pour water that has just started bubbling over the leaves. For green tea, let the water cool for a few minutes first before pouring it into the teapot. Remove strainer after $2\frac{1}{2}$ minutes (for green tea or stimulating black tea) or 5 minutes (for calming black tea).

Crispy Spring Rolls with Shrimp Filling
Finger food to die for

Feeds 4 for munching:

24 frozen spring roll wrappers
(about 8-inch squares; freeze the rest
of the package for future use)

2 oz. cellophane (mung bean thread) noodles

4 green onions

12 fresh chive spears

1 lb. peeled cooked shrimp, thawed

1 tablespoon fish sauce

½ teaspoon hot chili oil (optional)

1 pinch sugar

Salt (if needed)

4¼ cups vegetable oil for deep-frying

For the sauce:

1–2 fresh red chiles (Fresno=mild,
red jalapeño or serrano=hot)

2 cloves garlic

2 tablespoons fresh lime juice

1 tablespoon rice vinegar

1 teaspoon sugar

1 tablespoon fish sauce

1 tablespoon soy sauce

1 Thaw package of spring roll wrappers completely before opening. Place 24 wrappers on the table (wrap and freeze rest). Cover with a damp dishtowel to prevent drying. Place cellophane noodles in a bowl, pour hot tap water over the top and soak until soft. This takes about 10 minutes, but it won't hurt to leave them in the water longer.

2 Trim root end and any wilted parts from green onions. Rinse the rest and chop very finely. Rinse chives, shake dry and cut into ½-inch pieces. Dice cooked shrimp very finely. In the meantime, the noodles have had enough time to soften. Drain and cut into small pieces with kitchen scissors.

3 Mix all chopped ingredients in a bowl. Pour in fish sauce, hot chili oil and sugar, and stir. If desired, add a little salt but remember the fish sauce is also salty.

4 Now you're ready to roll: Lay a wrapper on a cutting board or directly on top of the working surface. Spread some filling on the side closest to you, leaving some margin (in the shape of a short log). Fold the edge closest to you over the filling and roll up one turn. Then fold in the right and left edges over the filling and finish rolling it up, away from you. In the same way fill and roll all the other wrappers and arrange them side by side on a platter.

5 Heat oil in a high-sided pot to 350–375°F (use an oil thermometer to test). Other ways to test the oil: Stick the handle of a wooden spoon down into the oil—if bubbles congregate around the handle, it's ready. Or, throw in a cube of white bread—it should turn brown and crispy within 1 minute.

6 Meanwhile, prepare the sauce: Rinse chile peppers and remove stems. For less heat, remove ribs and seeds. (Always wear gloves when working with hot peppers.) Peel garlic and mince along with the chiles. Stir together lime juice, rice vinegar and sugar until sugar is dissolved. Add in fish sauce, soy sauce, garlic and chiles. Transfer sauce to four small bowls.

7 Then place about one fourth of the spring rolls in the hot oil with a slotted spoon and deep-fry for about 3–4 minutes, and until golden. Cover a large platter with a triple layer of paper towels. Remove spring rolls from oil with the slotted metal utensil and drain on the paper towels. Fry remaining spring rolls and serve with sauce for dipping.

Prep time: 1 hour
Calories per serving: 360

Some Additional Fillings:

Chicken Vegetable Filling

Finely chop ½ lb. chicken breast and ⅔ lb. rinsed vegetables (e.g., daikon, carrots, white cabbage, green onions) and fry in 2 tablespoons oil for about 5 minutes along with 1 piece (¾-inch section) peeled and minced ginger and 1–2 finely diced jalapeños (hot) or red Fresno chiles (mild). Stir in 4 oz. crumbled tofu and a few sprigs of chopped cilantro. Season to taste with salt and pepper, roll up in the wrappers and deep-fry until golden brown and crispy.

Ground Pork Filling

Peel and finely chop 1 piece (¾-inch section) ginger and 4 cloves garlic. Rinse 5 green onions, trim wilted parts and chop rest. Rinse ½ cup fresh mint sprigs, shake dry and finely chop. Mix chopped ingredients into ¾ lb. ground pork and ½ lb. bean sprouts and season with salt. Roll up in the wrappers and deep-fry until golden brown and crispy.

Vegetarian Filling

Soak 4–6 dried mushrooms in warm water for about 30 minutes, then remove stems and finely chop mushroom caps. Soak 2 oz. cellophane (mung bean thread) noodles in hot tap water until softened and then cut into small pieces. Rinse and chop 1 cup spinach leaves and ½ lb. Chinese (napa) cabbage and sauté in 1 tablespoon oil until softened. Crumble 8 oz. tofu. Combine all these ingredients with ½ tablespoon cornstarch. Season with 1 tablespoon oyster sauce, 1 tablespoon soy sauce, 2 teaspoons sesame oil and a little salt and pepper. Roll up in the wrappers and deep-fry until golden brown and crispy. Mix a little freshly grated ginger and hot chili oil into a little soy sauce—serve alongside vegetable spring rolls for dipping.

Basic Tip

The spring roll wrappers are so moist that they usually stick together well after rolling. But if they don't, you can create a natural glue: Mix together 1 tablespoon cornstarch and 1½ tablespoons water to form a paste. Brush paste onto the ends of the wrappers for pressing together. Also, it's a good idea to set the oven to about 170°F to keep the finished spring rolls warm while you're deep- frying the rest of the batches.

Lettuce Wraps
Guest-participation food

Feeds 6 as an appetizer or 4 as a very light lunch:

3½ oz. cellophane (mung bean thread) noodles

1 lb. cooked chicken (cooked with the Chinese chicken stock on pages 58–59 or buy pre-cooked)

½ lb. surimi (also called imitation crab, kamaboko)

1 cucumber

2 carrots

1 ripe avocado

6 green onions

¾ cup fresh mint sprigs

¾ cup fresh basil sprigs

⅔ cup roasted salted peanuts

½ cup bean sprouts

1 head iceberg or 2 heads butter, (or bibb) lettuce

For the sauce:

¼ cup sugar

½ cup soy sauce

½ cup rice vinegar

Optional condiments for the table:

Chile-garlic sauce, soy sauce, sesame oil, Japanese pickled ginger

1 Soak cellophane noodles in hot tap water for about 10 minutes. Tear chicken into fine strips. Slice surimi thinly.

2 Rinse cucumber, remove ends and halve lengthwise. Scrape out seeds with a spoon and slice rest crosswise thinly. Peel carrots; first cut lengthwise into thin slices and then into fine strips. Halve avocado, remove pit and cut flesh into thin wedges. Remove roots and any wilted parts from green onions, rinse, cut into pieces 1½ inches long and then into fine strips.

3 Rinse herbs, shake dry and discard any tough stems. Chop nuts. Rinse bean sprouts. Remove lettuce leaves from head, rinse and pat dry. For the sauce, mix sugar, soy sauce and vinegar; heat only to dissolve sugar. Place all ingredients on the table.

4 For the meal, each person lays one lettuce leaf on a plate, fills it with ingredients as desired, rolls it up and dips it in the sauce (or uses optional condiments).

Prep time: 45 minutes
Calories per serving (4): 650

Fresh Tofu Spring Rolls
Tender Vietnamese treat

Feeds 4 as a starter:

16 dried rice paper wrappers, (8½-inch diameter)

8 lettuce leaves

8 oz. firm tofu

1 tablespoon fish sauce

Chili powder

½ cup vegetable oil for pan-frying

4 white (green) cabbage leaves

½ cup bean sprouts

½ cup fresh mint sprigs

½ cup fresh cilantro sprigs

For the sauce:

1 fresh red chile (Fresno, serrano, or jalapeño)

2 cloves garlic

1 piece ginger (¾-inch section)

2 tablespoons roasted salted peanuts

1 teaspoon sugar

2 tablespoons fish sauce

1 tablespoon soy sauce

1 tablespoon rice vinegar

1 Fill a large bowl with lukewarm water. Dip rice paper wrappers one at a time until pliable. Remove, lay side by side on a work surface and cover with a damp dishtowel.

2 Rinse lettuce leaves, pat dry and pare down any thick ribs (flatten leaves). Cut tofu into strips ½ inch thick; brush with fish sauce and dust with chili powder. Pat dry. Heat oil in a pan and fry tofu strips until golden. Drain on paper towels.

3 Rinse cabbage leaves, sprouts, mint and cilantro; drain all. Cut cabbage into strips. Trim away tough stems from herbs.

4 Stack rice paper wrappers two high, top with 1 lettuce leaf and some each of the tofu, cabbage, sprouts and herbs. Fold wrapper edges over the filling and roll up the rice paper wrappers tightly. Arrange on a platter.

5 For the dipping sauce, rinse chile pepper and remove stem (always wear gloves when working with hot peppers, and don't touch your face); mince rest. Omit seeds and ribs for less heat. Peel garlic and ginger; finely chop along with peanuts. Mix sugar, fish sauce, soy sauce and rice vinegar; stir in chile, garlic, ginger and peanuts. Serve with spring rolls.

Prep time: 50 minutes
Delicious followed by: Red Chicken Curry (page 143) and Mango Cream (page 155)
Calories per serving: 285

Stuffed Rice Paper Treats with Dip
With an extra crunch!

Feeds 8 as an appetizer:

¾ lb. ground chicken breast

1 leek

½ lb. ground pork

3 tablespoons soy sauce

1 tablespoon cornstarch

½ cup peanuts or cashews

¾ cup sprigs fresh cilantro

16 rice paper wrappers (6-inch diameter)

1 egg white

4 ¼ cups oil for deep-frying

For the dip:

1 chunk daikon (about ¼ lb.)

1 piece ginger (¾-inch section)

2 fresh red Fresno chiles (mild to medium)

2 teaspoons sugar

3 tablespoons ketchup

1½ tablespoons fish sauce

1 tablespoon soy sauce

1 Trim root end and any wilted parts from leek, slit open lengthwise and rinse well; chop finely. Mix chicken, leek, ground pork, soy sauce and cornstarch. Add a little salt. Chop nuts finely. Rinse cilantro, shake dry and chop finely.

2 For the dip, peel daikon and ginger and grate both. Rinse chiles, remove stems and mince—for less heat, omit seeds. Mix sugar, ketchup, fish sauce, soy sauce, daikon, ginger and red chiles; transfer dip to individual serving bowls.

3 Fill a large bowl with warm water. Dip rice paper wrappers one at a time until pliable. Lay each on a work surface. Spread meat mixture on half the wrappers, leaving a one-inch margin around the edges. Sprinkle with nuts and cilantro. Brush egg white on the edges, lay remaining rice paper wrappers on top and press edges together well.

4 Set oven to 170°F and place a large paper towel-lined platter inside. Heat oil in a large pan to 350–375°F. One rice treat will need to be able to fit down into the pan. To test the oil: lower the handle of a wooden spoon down into it—if tiny bubbles congregate around it, it's time. Deep-fry one of the rice paper treats for 2 minutes, turn with metal tongs and fry another 1½ minutes. Remove and drain on the prepared platter and keep warm in the oven. Repeat the process with the rest.

5 Each person cuts theirs into wedges or strips and eats it with the dip.

Prep time: 1 hour
Calories per serving: 405

Dim Sum
Don't forget to soak rice the night before

Feeds 6 or 8:

For the rice balls:

$^2/_3$ cup short- or medium-grain rice

2 cloves garlic

1 piece ginger ($^3/_4$-inch section)

1 tablespoon chopped fresh cilantro

1 lb. lean ground pork

1 egg white

3 tablespoons soy sauce

1 tablespoon rice wine (mirin)

1 teaspoon sugar

For the dumplings:

2 cups flour, plus a little more

for rolling out dough

$^1/_2$ tablespoon butter

Salt

5–6 dried shiitake mushrooms

1 small head Chinese (napa) cabbage

2 tablespoons vegetable oil

2 tablespoons rice wine

2 tablespoons soy sauce

2 teaspoons sesame oil

$^1/_2$ teaspoon hot chile oil

1 For the rice balls: rinse rice in a fine mesh strainer, pour into a bowl and cover with water. Soak overnight.

2 The next day, start with the dumplings: Mix flour together with butter, salt and at least 6 tablespoons warm water; knead briefly. Roll into a ball, cover with a cloth, and let stand for at least 30 minutes. Soak mushrooms in hot tap water for 30 minutes.

3 For the rice balls: Peel garlic and mince; peel ginger and grate. Rinse cilantro, shake dry, and mince. Mix together garlic, ginger, cilantro, pork, egg white, soy sauce, rice wine and sugar; shape into walnut-sized balls. Drain soaked rice and distribute on a plate. Roll balls in the rice until covered on all sides. Place in a bamboo steamer (preferably two-tiered) and cover.

4 For the dumplings, rinse Chinese (napa) cabbage and chop. Drain and rinse mushrooms; pat dry. Discard stems and slice caps. Stir-fry cabbage and mushrooms in oil for about 5 minutes. Pour in rice wine and turn off heat. Season to taste with soy sauce, sesame oil and hot chile oil.

5 Knead dumpling dough once again and pinch off walnut-sized pieces. Roll out each piece on a lightly floured work surface until thin and round. Place a little filling in the middle and close dough over the top, twisting slightly. Leave dumplings on the work surface, covered with a dishtowel.

6 For steaming rice balls and dumplings, fill a large pot or wok (the steamer bottom must fit inside) with 1 inch deep of water and bring to a boil. Place bamboo steamer with rice balls in the pot, cover and steam over medium heat for 30 minutes, checking periodically to maintain water level. If necessary, add a little hot water to pot or wok.

7 Remove rice balls and place dumplings in the steamer. Steam for about 10 minutes. In the meantime, start eating the rice balls.

Prep time: 1/2 hours (plus overnight soaking and 30 minutes steaming)
Delicious with: Chile-garlic sauce, sweet chile sauce (page 57), soy sauce mixed with rice vinegar and grated ginger, sesame oil or pure soy sauce
Calories per serving (6): 355

Five-Spice
Fish Fillets
Really easy

Feeds 4 as a small appetizer:

1 lb. thin fish fillets (e.g., trout, sole, snapper)

$1/4$ cup rice wine (sake, mirin)

Salt

1 piece ginger ($1/2$-inch section)

4 cloves garlic

2 tablespoons vegetable oil

2 tablespoons soy sauce

1 teaspoon sugar

1 teaspoon five-spice powder

5 green onions

1 teaspoon sesame oil

1 Check the fish fillets for bones and remove any you find with tweezers. Then cut fillets into bite-size pieces. Combine rice wine with a little salt and distribute evenly on all sides of the fish. Cover and marinate in the refrigerator for at least 30 minutes or longer.

2 Peel ginger and garlic and mince both. Heat oil in a pan or wok. Sauté fish pieces very briefly (to sear) and remove from oil (these will be cooked more later). Sauté garlic and ginger in this same oil. Add 1 cup water, soy sauce, sugar and five-spice powder, and bring to a boil. Place fish in this liquid and simmer uncovered for about 10 minutes.

3 Meanwhile, trim root ends and any wilted parts from green onions; rinse and slice into fine rings. Remove fish from cooking liquid and transfer to individual plates (warm plates first in a 170°F oven). Ladle some cooking liquid over the top, sprinkle with green onions, and drizzle with sesame oil to serve.

Prep time: 1 hour
(15 minutes of which you're actually busy)
Delicious with: Chinese pancakes (page 142) and cucumber slices
Calories per serving: 245

Tip:
As the name "five-spice powder" implies, this seasoning contains five spices—usually cinnamon, fennel, anise, pepper and cloves. If you want, you can also mix the whole seeds yourself and crush them finely with a mortar and pestle or in a grinder dedicated to spices.

Instead of cucumber slices, this dish also tastes great with a **Spicy Cucumber Salad:** Remove seeds from 1 peeled cucumber and slice. Combine with 1 red onion cut into strips and 2 fresh red Fresno chile peppers cut into rings. Bring to a boil $1/3$ cup rice vinegar, $1/3$ cup water, 1 tablespoon sugar and a pinch salt; add in cucumbers, red onions and chiles.

Clams in
Sake Sauce
Ready in a flash

Feeds 4 as a starter:

$2^{1}/_{4}$ lbs. clams

1 piece ginger ($3/4$-inch section)

1 clove garlic

2 green onions

1 tablespoon vegetable oil

1 cup rice wine (sake)

3 tablespoons soy sauce

1 teaspoon sugar

1 Rinse clams thoroughly under cold running water. If they're very dirty, scrub with a brush. Make sure the clams close when you rinse them. Discard any that don't.

2 Peel ginger and garlic, cut both into paper-thin slices and then into very fine strips. Remove root ends and any wilted parts from green onions, rinse and slice rest thinly into rings.

3 Heat oil in a large pot or wok. Briefly sauté ginger, garlic and green onions. Add sake, soy sauce and sugar and bring to a boil. Then add clams and cover immediately. Cook clams over high heat for 3–5 minutes, until most of them open. If necessary, cook for a brief period longer to allow more to open.

4 Important: throw away any clams that don't open. Serve clams with the cooking liquid.

Prep time: 30 minutes
Delicious with: Japanese pickled ginger, individual bowls of short- or medium-grain rice, any Asian-inspired entrée
Calories per serving: 145

Tuna with Wasabi Sauce
Pretty and delicious

Feeds 4 as a starter or a snack:

1 chunk daikon (2-inch section)

1 tablespoon sesame seeds

$\frac{1}{4}$ cup soy sauce

$\frac{1}{2}$–1 teaspoon wasabi (from a tube)

1 sheet nori (toasted seaweed, Japanese grocery)

$\frac{1}{2}$ lb. sushi-grade ahi tuna

1 Peel daikon and slice paper-thin or grate. Arrange on four small plates.

2 Toast sesame seeds in a dry pan while stirring constantly until they give off a roasted aroma and are a pale golden color. Crush as finely as possible in a grinder or mortar and pestle. In a small bowl, combine crushed sesame with soy sauce and wasabi. Cut nori sheet into long slivers and then shorter strips (it's easiest using kitchen scissors).

3 First slice tuna thinly, then cut into very fine strips. Lay on top of daikon slices and garnish with nori strips. Drizzle with wasabi sauce and serve.

Prep time: 20 minutes
Delicious followed by: Teriyaki Duck (page 143) or Sukiyaki (page 130)
Calories per serving: 255

Variation:

Tuna with Sesame Sauce
In Korea, tuna is also eaten like this:

Rinse 1 small cucumber, halve, remove seeds and cut rest into fine strips. Rinse 2 green onions, remove root end and any wilted parts and slice rest into rings. Mix cucumber and green onions with 1 tablespoon chopped, roasted salted peanuts. Cut $\frac{2}{3}$ lb. sushi-grade tuna, first into the thinnest possible slices, then into tiny cubes. Distribute on plates along with the cucumber mixture. Boil $\frac{1}{2}$ cup chicken stock and mix with 3 tablespoons soy sauce, 1 teaspoon sesame oil, 1 tablespoon toasted sesame seeds, 2 teaspoons sugar and 2 garlic cloves squeezed through a press. Let cool and drizzle over tuna.

Chinese Sesame-Chicken Salad
Simply splendid and authentically Chinese

Feeds 4:

1 lb. chicken breast fillets

Salt

1 cucumber

1 fresh red Fresno chile

2 tablespoons oil

1/2 teaspoon crushed red pepper flakes

2 teaspoons Sichuan peppercorns

For the dressing:

1/4 cup sesame seeds

3 tablespoons soy sauce

2 teaspoons sesame oil

1 1/2 tablespoons peanut oil

1 teaspoon sugar

1 Place chicken in a pot, cover with water (or chicken stock), add salt and bring to a boil slowly, starting with medium heat. Then cover and simmer over low heat for about 10 minutes. Pierce fillets with a knife. If clear juice runs out, they're done. If the juice is still pink, let them go for a few more minutes until cooked throughout. Then let chicken cool in the liquid.

2 Meanwhile, rinse cucumber, trim ends and halve lengthwise. Scrape out seeds with a spoon and cut cucumber into narrow strips (about 4 inches long). Rinse fresh chile, discard stem and chop rest.

3 Heat oil in a pan or wok and sauté chile and Sichuan peppercorns briefly. Add cucumber strips and sauté on medium-high heat for about 2 minutes. Season with salt, transfer to a plate and let cool.

4 Remove chicken from cooking liquid, drain and tear into fine strips. Arrange cucumber mixture on a platter or four plates and then top with chicken.

5 For the sauce, toast sesame seeds in a dry pan until a pale golden color. Grind in a spice mill or small food processor. Whisk together sesame seeds, soy sauce, sesame oil, peanut oil and sugar. If the sauce is too thick, add a tiny bit of water. Drizzle over the salads and serve (either at room temperature or chilled).

Prep time: 30 minutes
Calories per serving: 390

Another Dressing Option:

Vinegar Ginger Sauce
Peel 1 piece ginger (3/4-inch section) and 2 cloves garlic and mince or grate both. Rinse 2 green onions, discard wilted parts and chop rest very finely. Combine 3 tablespoons rice vinegar, 3 tablespoons soy sauce and 2 teaspoons sesame oil. Mix in ginger, garlic and green onions and serve over Chinese chicken salad.

Basic Tip
The chicken breast fillet will be even more tender if you steam it instead of boiling. Drizzle the meat with a little rice wine, place it in a steamer and top with a few thin strips of leek (rinsed well) and slices of fresh ginger. In a covered pot, steam over boiling water for about 10 minutes. Chicken is done when it's opaque throughout, and when juices run clear upon piercing with a paring knife.

Lemon Grass Seafood Skewers
Impressive and addictive

Feeds 4:

1 piece ginger (½-inch section)

1 fresh red Fresno chile pepper

4–5 sprigs fresh cilantro

½ lb. fish fillets (e.g., cod, sole, snapper, pollock)

½ lb. peeled raw shrimp

⅓ cup coconut milk

1 egg white

Salt

12 stalks lemon grass

4¼ cups oil for deep-frying

For the sauce:

1¾ cups pineapple chunks (fresh or canned)

4 green onions

2 cloves garlic

1 tablespoon oil

1 teaspoon sugar

3 tablespoons rice vinegar

Salt

1 teaspoon sambal oelek (Asian grocery)

1 tablespoon fresh lime or lemon juice

1 For the sauce, dice pineapple finely. Remove roots, any wilted parts and dark green tops from green onions; rinse rest and chop. Peel garlic and mince. Sauté garlic and green onions briefly in oil. Mix sugar, rice vinegar and salt; add to garlic and green onions along with pineapple, sambal oelek and citrus juice.

2 For the skewers, first peel ginger. Rinse chile pepper and discard stem. Rinse cilantro and shake dry. Finely chop ginger, chile and cilantro together. Chop fish and shrimp coarsely. Purée fish and shrimp in a blender or food processor along with coconut milk and egg white. Stir in ginger, chile pepper and cilantro; add a little salt.

3 Rinse lemon grass. Divide seafood mixture into 12 portions. Moisten your hands and shape each portion into a rectangle. Then place 1 lemon grass stalk on the rectangle and wrap the seafood mixture around the stalk, attempting to achieve an even thickness all around.

4 Heat frying oil to 350–375°F (use an oil thermometer). Deep-fry skewers for 4–5 minutes or until cooked through and the seafood mixture is golden brown; drain on a paper towel-lined platter and serve alongside sauce.

Prep time: 35 minutes
Delicious followed by: Stir-Fried Beef and Rice Noodles (page 82) or Squid Curry (page 114)
Calories per serving: 330

Vegetable Pakoras
How vegetables are packaged in India

Feeds 4 as an appetizer:

2⅔ cups chickpea flour (specialty store)

Salt

1 teaspoon vegetable oil plus 4¼ cups for deep-frying

2 jalapeños

½ cup fresh mint sprigs

1 cup (8 oz.) yogurt

½ teaspoon ground cumin

1¾ lbs. vegetables (e.g., potatoes, cauliflower, broccoli, eggplant, zucchini)

A few uncooked shrimp (optional), peeled and deveined

1 For the batter, combine chickpea flour with a few pinches salt. Add 1 teaspoon vegetable oil to 1 cup lukewarm water and whisk mixture into chickpea flour until it forms a thick liquid batter. Set aside.

2 For the yogurt dip, rinse jalapeños, remove stem and chop rest (omit seeds and ribs for less heat). Always wear gloves when working with hot peppers and don't touch

your face. Rinse mint, shake dry and chop coarsely. Purée yogurt, mint and jalapeños in a blender or food processor. Season dip to taste with salt and cumin.

3 Peel or rinse vegetables and cut into bite-size chunks (don't cut potatoes any thicker than ¼-inch). Rinse shrimp and pat dry.

4 Set oven to 170°F and warm a large platter, lined with paper towels, inside. Heat the 4¼ cups oil, in a high-sided pot, to 350–375°F (use an oil thermometer). Or, to test whether it's hot enough, stick the handle of a wooden spoon into the oil. If bubbles congregate around the handle, it's ready.

5 Gradually dip vegetables (and shrimp if using) in the batter to coat (if it's too thick, whisk in more lukewarm water). Deep-fry pieces in the hot oil for about 4 minutes and until golden. Remove from oil with a slotted metal utensil, drain on paper towel-lined platter and then keep warm in the oven until remaining vegetables are fried. Serve yogurt dip alongside.

Prep time: 35 minutes
Delicious followed by: Tandoori Chicken (page 140), Saffron Almond Rice (page 77) and chutney (Mango Chutney, page 75; Coconut Chutney, page 94)
Calories per serving: 380

Tamarind Fried Shrimp
Typical Southeast Asian

Feeds 4:

1 tablespoon tamarind paste

2 red onions

5 cloves garlic

1 fresh red chile pepper or ½ teaspoon crushed red pepper flakes

1 lb. uncooked, peeled and de-veined shrimp

4¼ cups vegetable oil for deep-frying

1 tablespoon brown sugar

2 teaspoons fish sauce

1 teaspoon rice vinegar

1 egg white

Salt

2 tablespoons cornstarch

1 Stir tamarind paste into ½ cup hot tap water; set aside. Peel onions and garlic; chop both finely. Rinse chile pepper, remove stem and chop finely (always wear gloves when working with hot peppers). Remove tails from shrimp; rinse and pat dry (if using frozen shrimp, thaw first according to package directions). Set shrimp aside.

2 Heat oil in a pot to 350–375°F, testing with an oil thermometer (you can also test by inserting the end of a wooden spoon— bubbles should rise to the surface). Meanwhile, for the sauce: combine onions, garlic, chile, tamarind mixture and brown sugar in a pot; bring to a boil, then reduce heat and simmer for about 5 minutes. Add fish sauce and rice vinegar, stir and turn off heat. Sauce is finished.

3 Combine egg white and salt and dip each shrimp in this mixture. Then dust lightly with cornstarch using a small, fine-mesh strainer. Deep-fry shrimp in hot oil for about 2 minutes or until golden. Remove with a metal slotted spoon (or other metal utensil), drain briefly on a paper towel-lined platter, and serve immediately with the sauce.

Prep time: 50 minutes
Calories per serving: 245

Chirashi Sushi
Scattered instead of pressed

Place sushi rice in a bowl, spread the filling on top and you're done!

Feeds 4 or even 6:

½ cucumber

½ teaspoon salt

3 eggs

1 tablespoon sugar

1 tablespoon Japanese soy sauce

1 tablespoon rice wine (mirin, sake)

2 teaspoons oil

8 peeled, *cooked* shrimp

2 sheets nori (toasted seaweed)

1 batch sushi rice (see Tip page 53)

1 piece ginger (1-inch section)

8 lemon wedges

1 Peel cucumber, quarter lengthwise and remove seeds with a spoon. Slice cucumber quarters and combine with salt. Drain cucumber slices in a colander for about 30 minutes.

2 In the meantime, mix together eggs, sugar, soy sauce and rice wine. In a small nonstick pan, heat 1 teaspoon of the oil.

Cook half the egg mixture over low heat until the underside is set, turn omelet and finish cooking, trying not to let it brown. Make a second omelet with the remaining oil and egg mixture. Roll up both, let cool and slice thinly.

3 Halve shrimp lengthwise. Using kitchen scissors, cut nori sheets into ½-inch squares. Mix sushi rice and cucumber and distribute in four small bowls. Sprinkle with cooked shrimp, egg pieces and nori. Peel ginger and finely grate—sprinkle over the top. Serve with lemon wedges.

Prep time: 40 minutes
Calories per serving (6): 315

Onigiri
Homemade sushi

Basic Cooking tells you how to make maki or nigiri sushi (page 104). Here, we bring you a version of onigiri sushi that can be prepared at home.

Feeds 8 as a starter:

6 tablespoons sesame seeds

10–12 oz. non-raw fish (e.g., water-packed tuna, smoked salmon, cooked shrimp)

2 tablespoons Japanese pickled ginger

5 sheets seasoned, roasted nori (seaweed)

¼ cup red caviar (traditionally tabuko from flying fish)

1 batch sushi rice (see p. 53)

⅓ cup rice vinegar for shaping

Japanese soy sauce and wasabi (from a tube), for dipping

1 Toast sesame seeds in a dry pan and set aside. Break fish into small pieces. Chop pickled ginger. Coarsely crumble 1 sheet nori with your fingers (use a plastic bag to minimize waste). Cut remaining sheets into strips ½ inch wide using kitchen scissors.

2 Loosely mix together fish, crumbled nori, pickled ginger, 2 tablespoons of the toasted sesame seeds, 2 tablespoons of the caviar and sushi rice. Combine ⅓ cup water and the rice vinegar; use to moisten your hands.

3 Take walnut-sized portions of rice mixture, and form into balls. Roll balls in remaining sesame seeds and wrap each ball once around with a nori strip, shiny side out. Garnish the top of each ball with caviar. Stir together soy sauce and wasabi and dip the onigiri into this sauce.

Prep time: 30 minutes
Calories per serving: 570

Temaki Sushi
Hand-rolled

It looks like more work than it actually is, because, you prepare all the ingredients first and let your guests do the rest at the table.

Makes 16 sushi rolls:

3 eggs

3 teaspoons sugar

2 tablespoons Japanese soy sauce,

plus more for dipping

1 teaspoon vegetable oil

4 green onions

1 ripe avocado

1/2 cucumber

5 oz. tofu

1/2 teaspoon fresh lemon juice

1/2 cup bean sprouts

8 large sheets seasoned, roasted nori (seaweed)

1 batch sushi rice (see Tip, this page)

Wasabi (from a tube) and mayonnaise

for spreading

1/3 cup rice wine for shaping

1 Mix eggs, sugar and 1 tablespoon of the soy sauce. Place mixture in a small nonstick

pan brushed with the oil; cover and cook over the lowest possible heat for 5 minutes until set. Flip in pan, turn off heat and let cool.

2 Rinse green onions, trim root end and any wilted parts, and cut lengthwise into quarters. Cut avocado in half, remove pit, scoop out flesh and and slice into 1/2-inch x 2-inch strips. Peel cucumber, halve lengthwise and remove seeds. Slice tofu and omelet into 1/2-inch x 2-inch strips.

3 Soak green onions in ice water for 15 minutes; drain. Mix avocado with lemon juice and mix tofu with the remaining 1 tablespoon soy sauce. Rinse sprouts and drain. Cut nori sheets in half using kitchen shears. Place all prepared ingredients on the table plus the sushi rice, wasabi and mayonnaise. Also supply each guest with small saucers of water and rice wine for shaping, plus a plate or cutting board.

4 Each guest should: Lay nori sheets on the board, shiny side down. Using a wet spoon, spread the left half with a thin layer of sushi rice. Spread rice with wasabi and/or mayonnaise and lay a few strips of desired ingredients diagonally on top. Then roll the nori around the filling tightly into a little cone and use a dab of water to press it together. Drizzle with soy sauce and eat out of hand.

Prep time: 30 minutes
(plus hand-rolling at the table)
Calories per serving: 140

Basic Tip
Sushi Rice

Swish around 1³/4 cup sushi rice (short- or medium-grain) in a bowl of cold water. Drain and repeat 5 times or until water is nearly clear. Let drain in a colander for 1 hour. Then bring rice and 2 cups + 2 tablespoons water to a boil over high heat. Reduce heat to very low and add 1/3 cup cold water. Cover and cook for 5 more minutes. Remove from heat, uncover and let sit for 10 minutes. Transfer to a bowl, fluff with a wooden spoon, and let cool. Bring 1/4 cup rice vinegar to a boil with salt and 3 teaspoons sugar. Gradually add to lukewarm rice. Salt to taste. Use for making sushi.

Prep time: 45 minutes (not including draining time)

Soups &

Slurp, please, and pay attention to detail...

Salads

Remember the introduction to the second chapter in Basic Cooking under "Salads & Soups" where it says, "People who make good salads have an eye for detail," and "People who make good soup know what's important"?

In Asian cuisine, both soups and salads rely on detail, and they're both important, even if what they play is really a supporting role. Once they're made, details go out the window and it's time to eat them with abandon.

Salads like those in Thailand that combine fresh herbs, fish sauce, palm sugar and hot chiles are so good, they're unique in all the world. And how else could such apparently simple dishes like Japanese miso soup or Chinese chicken noodle soup leave behind such a powerful impression? But don't be overly respectful of them—they're really just something to slurp. And slurping is expressly encouraged in Asia when eating a noodle soup.

Finger Exercise No. 2
Garnishing with Radish Stems

As you master this exercise, the first two steps will increase your appreciation for precision and the second stage will strengthen your appreciation for patience.

1. Clean the thinner stems from a bunch of radishes, preferably white radishes (beet stems also work), and lay them between two wooden or bamboo skewers. Then score the stems down to the skewers at an angle and at intervals of about ¼ inch, using a paring knife or bird's beak knife.

2. Now score each stem lengthwise almost to the ends (but not all the way through). Place them in cold water with ice cubes and refrigerate.

3. Wait patiently for half a day. If everything went well, the garnishes will already be curling up in the water. They look super in salads and with cold appetizers.

Dear Aunt Betty,

My friends and I are now in Vietnam, sitting at a laminate table in a fast-food restaurant in Saigon. You get the picture. And we just noticed that the beef noodle soup mom used to make is nothing compared to what they have here! In the hotel they told us to ask for "pho." That's what we did and here came this giant bowl of extremely white rice noodles with raw and cooked beef in it. Luckily the guy from the hotel appeared just at that moment and showed us what to do. First we added a few spoonfuls and dashes from the bowls and bottles on the table (the fish sauce is called "nuoc nam," and it's amazing). Then we used chopsticks to slurp up the noodles. Naturally, you have to throw your T-shirt in the wash afterwards, but it was fantastic. Those slippery, slurpy noodles, that broth—all of it simply fabulous! Now he's asking whether we want a Durian for dessert. I don't even know what that is! What an adventure—gotta go!

See you,
Your niece, Elaine

To:
Aunt Betty
123 Homesick Lane
Des Moines, Iowa
United States

12.06.2002
POST
Basic Services

5

Homemade Asian Basics
Chile Sauce

More specifically, sweet chile sauce. In Asia you can buy it by the liter (about a quart), but that's only for hardcore hot sauce lovers. A small bottle of homemade sauce will be enough for you to start. Thanks to its spiciness, and the vinegar in the recipe, this sauce keeps for a very long time in the refrigerator.

Rinse 6–8 long, red serrano chile peppers (Asian grocery). Halve lengthwise. Depending on how hot you want the sauce, remove the seeds and ribs (milder—but still hot) or leave them in (hotter). Always wear gloves when working with hot peppers, and don't touch your face.

Place peppers in a mortar with 1 teaspoon coarse sea salt and crush—don't worry if it still contains some larger pieces. Or use a small food processor.

Bring to a boil 2/3 cup sugar, 2/3 cup rice vinegar and 2/3 cup water; reduce to a light syrup. Meanwhile peel 4 cloves garlic and mince or crush.

Sauté garlic on very low heat in 1 tablespoon oil until lightly golden (30 seconds to 1 minute). Add garlic and chiles to syrup, transfer to a bottle and refrigerate. Use as a condiment at the table.

Drinking Asian Style:
Cocktails

Okay, a lot of things were invented in Asia but surely not the cocktail? Well, if you look past your images of rice terraces and colorful markets and to the more recent past, you'll discover a small bar culture in the Far East. In larger cities with ties to the West such as Shanghai and Singapore, bartenders have even come up with one or two world-famous classics—ever heard of a Singapore Sling?

The tropical drinks served at happy hour in Southeast Asia take on regional flavor when mixed for hammock-loungers. In such places the drinkers are usually from the West. What makes these drinks so wonderfully refreshing is the fresh juice from limes, passion fruit, pineapple or mangos. Coconut milk often is used to give substance and a luxurious texture. Rum or arrak supply the alcoholic content.

We don't know whether it was an Asian or American barkeep who invented the variety of martini made with Japanese rice wine known as a saketini, but we do know how it's made:

Saketini: Pour 2 tablespoons gin and 1 tablespoon sake over 5 ice cubes, shake if desired, and strain into a glass; serve with 1 green olive.

Singapore Sling: Pour 2 tablespoons gin, 2 teaspoons cherry brandy (kirsch), 1/3 cup Cointreau, 1/3 cup DOM benedictine liqueur, 2 teaspoons grenadine, 1/2 cup pineapple juice and 2 teaspoons lime juice over 5 ice cubes. Shake if desired; strain and serve with a pineapple chunk and a cherry.

Chinese Chicken Stock
For a change

Makes 2 quarts stock:
1 whole chicken (about 3 lbs.)
5 oz. bacon (or other smoked ham;
e.g., prosciutto)
1 leek, rinsed well and chopped coarsely
1 piece ginger (1½-inch section), peeled
and sliced
Zest of one orange
4–5 dried shiitake mushrooms, rinsed
1 star anise
1 teaspoon Sichuan peppercorns
2 tablespoons rice wine (sake, mirin)
Salt

1 Rinse chicken inside and out, drain, and place in a large pot. Place raw bacon beside it, cover both with about 2 quarts cold water, and heat.

2 Add the leek, ginger, orange zest, shiitakes, star anise and Sichuan peppercorns to the pot. Simmer stock over low heat (just below a boil) for 1¼ hours, partially covered. Season to taste with rice wine and salt.

3 Let chicken cool in the stock, then remove (cooked chicken meat can be used for other recipes, such as the ones on page 59). Pour stock through a fine mesh strainer and let cool to room temperature (discard the parts left in the strainer). Refrigerate stock. Remove any fat that forms on top. Stock is ready to be used—freeze any stock you don't intend to use immediately.

Prep time: 1¾ hours
Calories per 1 cup stock: 62

Delicious in Chicken Stock:

Vegetables and Mushrooms

Wipe off 4–6 shiitake mushrooms with paper towels, discard stems and cut caps into very fine strips. Rinse 1/4 head Chinese cabbage and cut into strips. Peel 2 carrots; first cut lengthwise into thin slices and then into fine matchsticks. Finely chop 4 oz. canned bamboo shoots. Bring 3 cups chicken stock to a boil with 1 tablespoon soy sauce and 1 tablespoon rice wine. Add all prepared ingredients and simmer for about 5 minutes until vegetables are crisp-tender. Whisk 1 teaspoon cornstarch into 1 tablespoon cold water, stir into the soup and bring to a boil. Sprinkle with chives or cilantro leaves and drizzle with sesame oil if desired.

Noodles and Chicken

Cook 3 1/2 oz. Chinese egg noodles in at least 3 cups stock according to the package directions. Chop a little cooked chicken (amount depends on how hungry you are) and add. Season with soy sauce and rice vinegar. Rinse 5 green onions, cut into fine rings and sprinkle on top. Drizzle with a little sesame oil.

Chicken and Spinach

Rinse 2 handfuls spinach, drain and remove any tough stems. Dice 8 oz. tofu and 1/2 lb. cooked chicken. Add all these ingredients to 3 cups chicken stock and bring to a boil until spinach wilts. Add 2 tablespoons rice vinegar and a little sugar; serve drizzled with sesame oil. You can also sprinkle with a few green onion rings or add a few drops of hot chile oil.

Meatballs and Noodles

In a bowl, combine 1/2 lb. ground pork, 2 finely chopped green onions, 1 piece of finely chopped ginger (1/2-inch section) and 2 garlic cloves squeezed through a press. Add 1 tablespoon rice wine, salt, pepper and a little sesame oil; mix all together well and form into small meatballs. Cook 5 oz. Chinese egg noodles in boiling water according to the package directions, rinse under cold water and drain. Pour boiling water over 2 tomatoes, peel and cut into eighths. Bring to a boil 1 quart (4 cups) stock. Add meatballs and "poach" (cook by simmering) over low heat for 5 minutes or until cooked through. Add noodles and tomatoes to stock, heat for about another 2 minutes and season to taste.

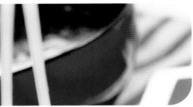

Japanese Dashi Stock
Few ingredients but lots of taste

This stock often appears in Japanese cookbooks. It's required not only for soups, including the famous Miso Soup (page 60), but also for many sauces.

Makes 1 quart stock:

1 sheet (1/3 oz.) kombu (dark, hard seaweed; Japanese market)

2 dried shiitake mushrooms

2 cups bonito flakes (smoked fish shavings; Japanese market)

1 Cut up kombu and mushrooms with kitchen scissors. This will help to release flavor during the short cooking time.

2 Place both ingredients in a pot with no more than 1 quart cold water and bring to a boil slowly over medium-high heat.

3 When the water is boiling, remove kombu and shiitake and add a shot of cold water so the stock will stop bubbling. Now add the bonito flakes and bring to a boil once again. Remove from heat, let stand briefly and pour through a fine mesh strainer. Ready to use.

Prep time: 15 minutes
Calories per serving: Not enough to worry about

Delicious in Dashi Stock:

Seafood Balls and Spinach

Coarsely chop 1/2 lb. fish fillets (e.g., sole, pollock or snapper) and/or peeled and de-veined raw shrimp. Purée in a blender. Combine with 1 egg white, 1 tablespoon rice wine (sake, mirin), 1 tablespoon cornstarch and 1 pinch sugar; form into small balls. Cook the balls in gently boiling water for about 2 minutes (or until cooked throughout), then remove. Heat 1 quart (4 cups) dashi stock. Rinse and then add: 1 handful snow peas, 1 thinly sliced carrot and 1 handful spinach, cooking until vegetables are crisp-tender. Season stock to taste with soy sauce, add cooked seafood balls and heat.

Mushrooms, Leek and Tofu

Wipe off 6 fresh shiitake mushrooms with paper towels, discard stems and slice caps thinly. Cut one leek into fine strips and rinse the strips very well in a tub of cold water. Finely dice 8 oz. firm tofu. Bring 1 quart dashi stock to a boil, season to taste with soy sauce and 2 tablespoons mirin (sweet Japanese rice wine), and cook mushrooms and leek in stock until leeks are crisp-tender. Add tofu and cook until heated through, then ladle soup into individual bowls.

Miso Soup
A Japanese treat

Feeds 4 as a small side dish:

8 oz. tofu

2 tender leeks (or even better, naganegi onions—Japanese grocery)

3 cups dashi stock (page 59 or instant)

3 oz. medium-dark miso

1 Cut tofu as uniformly as possible into ³/₄-inch cubes. Remove root end and darkest green parts from leeks, rinse rest, and slice on a slight diagonal into very thin rings. Rinse leek rings again, well, in a colander.

2 Heat dashi stock in a pot to just before boiling. Push miso through a strainer into the hot dashi; stir well. Do not allow to boil—very important.

3 Add tofu and leeks to pot; keep on heat for about 1 minute until both are warmed through. Serve miso soup.

Prep time: 10 minutes
Delicious with: A bowl of rice
Calories per serving: 100

Spicy-Sour Shrimp Soup
Thais know it as Tom Yum Goong

Feeds 4:

1 lb. uncooked shell-on shrimp

2 stalks lemon grass

1 tablespoon dried shrimp, (optional; Asian grocery)

2 tablespoons vegetable oil

²/₃ cup fresh cilantro sprigs

2 cloves garlic

¹/₈ teaspoon freshly ground black pepper

5 shiitake or oyster mushrooms

1 piece galangal (¹/₂-inch section; may substitute ginger)

2–4 fresh red chile peppers (Fresno=mild, jalapeño=hot, serrano=hotter)

¹/₄ cup fresh lime juice

4 kaffir lime leaves (Asian market or specialty store)

2 tablespoons fish sauce

1 teaspoon sugar

Salt

2 green onions

1 Peel shrimp by making a cut down the back using a small scissors. Also remove the dark vein. Rinse shrimp and halve lengthwise. Also rinse shells. Rinse 1 stalk lemon grass, remove outer layer, and cut rest into 1-inch sections.

2 In a pot, toast shrimp shells and dried shrimp in the oil. Add lemon grass and 1 quart water; bring to a boil. Then cook on medium-low for 15 minutes to create a shrimp stock. Meanwhile, rinse cilantro, shake dry and discard any tough stems. Peel garlic and coarsely chop. In a blender or small food processor, pulse the garlic, cilantro and black pepper (add a bit of water if necessary) to form a seasoning paste.

3 Discard mushroom stems; wipe off caps and thinly slice. Peel galangal and slice thinly. Rinse chiles, discard stems and cut rest into rings. Rinse remaining lemon grass and trim ends and remove outer later; slice the rest into fine rings.

4 Strain out the dried shrimp, shells and lemon grass from the stock and return the liquid to the pot. Add chiles, seasoning paste, lime juice, lemon grass rings, kaffir lime leaves, fish sauce and sugar; return to a boil.

5 Stir in galangal, mushrooms, and raw shrimp; cook over medium heat for 2 minutes. Salt soup to taste. Rinse green onions and slice white part into thin rings; use to garnish.

Prep time: 35 minutes
Delicious followed by: Red Chicken Curry (page 143) or Vegetables and Tofu in Coconut Milk (page 92)
Calories per serving: 170

Tomato Egg Flower Soup
Beautifully simple!

Feeds 4 or 6 as an appetizer:

1 piece ginger ($^1/_2$-inch section)

4 green onions

1 lb. tomatoes

1 tablespoon oil

1 tablespoon sugar

3 cups chicken stock (page 58 or purchased)

3 kaffir lime leaves (fresh or dried, Asian grocery)

$^1/_2$ cup fresh cilantro sprigs

3 eggs

Salt

Sesame oil for drizzling

1 Peel ginger and mince. Rinse green onions, trim root end and discard any wilted parts. Slice light green parts into rings; set aside. Halve the remaining white part and cut into fine strips.

2 Core tomatoes and pour boiling water over them in a bowl. Wait a moment, pour off water, peel tomatoes and cut into thin wedges.

3 Heat oil in a pot or wok and sauté the white green onion strips and ginger. Sprinkle with sugar and cook briefly on low until golden in color. Pour in stock, add kaffir lime leaves, heat and simmer gently for about 20 minutes.

4 Rinse cilantro, shake dry and discard stems. Whisk eggs with a little salt and pour into a small pitcher. Slowly pour egg mixture into soup. Let the soup rest for 30 seconds, then stir vigorously once with chopsticks. Season soup to taste with salt, sprinkle with green onion rings and cilantro leaves and drizzle with a couple drops of sesame oil before serving.

Prep time: 35 minutes, only 15 of which you're actually busy
Calories per serving (6): 330

Sweet Potato Spinach Soup
Malaysian combo

Feeds 4:

For the paste:

2 fresh red Fresno chile peppers (mildly hot)

4 shallots

$^2/_3$ cup grated coconut (unsweetened; available in health food stores)

$^1/_4$ teaspoon sugar

Salt

For the soup:

8 oz. baby spinach

1 medium-sized sweet potato (about $^1/_2$ lb.)

2 cloves garlic

1 jalapeño pepper

1 quart Chinese chicken stock (page 58 or purchased)

Soy sauce for seasoning

1 For the coconut paste, rinse Fresno chiles and discard stems. Peel shallots. Chop both ingredients coarsely, then purée in a blender along with grated coconut and sugar to form a paste. Season to taste with salt and pepper.

2 For the soup, sort spinach leaves, rinse in cold water, and drain in a colander. Peel sweet potatoes, cut into slices and then into matchsticks. Peel garlic and slice thinly. Rinse jalapeño, remove stem, seeds and ribs; cut rest into rings.

3 Heat stock. Add sweet potato, garlic, and jalapeño; simmer for about 5 minutes or until sweet potato is crisp-tender. Add spinach and cover and simmer until it slightly wilts. Season soup with soy sauce and serve with coconut paste as a condiment.

Prep time: 35 minutes
Calories per serving: 735

61

Ginger Soup with Duck and Asparagus
Luxury for more than one occasion

Feeds 4:

4 cloves garlic

1/2 cup fresh cilantro sprigs

2 tablespoons soy sauce

1 tablespoon honey

1 tablespoon rice vinegar

1/2 teaspoon sambal oelek (Asian grocery)

Salt

1 duck breast (about 3/4 lb.)

8 spears green asparagus

1 piece ginger (1-inch section)

1 quart chicken stock (page 58 or purchased)

2–3 teaspoons sesame oil

3/4 cup fresh basil sprigs (preferably Thai basil)

2 green onions

1 Peel garlic and squeeze through a press. Rinse cilantro, shake dry and chop leaves finely. Combine garlic and cilantro with 1 tablespoon of the soy sauce, the honey and the vinegar; season marinade to taste with sambal oelek and salt. Rub mixture onto duck breast, cover and marinate for 2 hours or longer.

2 Then heat the oven broiler. Remove duck breast from marinade, place on a rack over a baking sheet in the oven (center rack) and broil for about 15 minutes, turning occasionally. Remove and let cool a little.

3 Rinse asparagus and trim bottom ends. Cut off tips (reserve) and cut the rest on an angle into 1/2-inch pieces. Peel ginger and cut into slices, then into fine strips. Bring stock, ginger and sesame oil to a boil. Add asparagus and simmer for about 5 minutes until asparagus is crisp-tender.

4 Rinse basil, shake dry and strip off leaves. Remove roots and wilted parts from green onions, rinse rest and cut into fine rings. Slice duck breast thinly; add to stock mixture and heat through. Season soup to taste with soy sauce, sprinkle with basil and green onion rings and enjoy.

Prep time: 35 minutes
(plus 2 hours marinating time)
Delicious followed by: Fish Fillets with Asian Pesto (page 114) or Fried Rice (page 76)
Calories per serving: 765

Rice Noodle Soup with Pork
Indonesian-style

Feeds 4:

4 shallots

2 cloves garlic

2 jalapeños

1 teaspoon brown sugar

3 1/2 oz. wide rice noodles

Salt

3/4 lb. pork tenderloin or lean pork loin

3 tablespoons oil

1 tablespoon kecap manis
(sweet soy sauce, Asian grocery store)

1 quart chicken stock (page 58 or purchased)

2 tablespoons tamarind paste
(from container/jar, Asian grocery store)

3/4 cup bean sprouts

2 tablespoons fresh cilantro leaves

1/4 cup roasted salted peanuts, chopped

1 Peel shallots and garlic and chop both coarsely. Rinse jalapeños, discard stems and seeds, and chop rest coarsely. Purée shallots, garlic, jalapeños and brown sugar

62

using a hand blender, food processor or blender (use a bit of water if necessary).

2 Cook noodles until crisp-tender in lightly salted, boiling water (3–5 minutes). Drain and rinse with cold water.

3 Slice pork thinly (works best if slightly frozen). Heat 2 tablespoons of the oil in a wok or pan and sear meat briefly over high heat; remove from pan.

4 Heat remaining oil in pan and add the shallot purée; cook briefly. Season with kecap manis, pour in stock and bring to a boil. Add tamarind paste and return to a rolling boil.

5 Add sprouts (rinsed and drained) to soup along with pork and rice noodles; simmer for a couple minutes to heat ingredients through. Salt to taste and ladle into individual bowls. Garnish with cilantro and peanuts.

Prep time: 25 minutes
Calories per serving: 360

Also good:
Sprinkle soup with a little sugar and chili powder. And if you like the combined flavors of meat and fish together, purée 1–2 teaspoons shrimp paste with the shallots, garlic, chiles and brown sugar.

Coconut Soup with Chicken
Thai cuisine—so easy!

Feeds 4:

3/4 lb. chicken breast

2 tablespoons fish sauce

1 piece galangal (3/4-inch section;

may substitute ginger)

2 stalks lemon grass

1 red Fresno chile pepper (mildly hot)

4 firm medium tomatoes

1 can coconut milk (1 2/3 cups)

2 1/4 cups chicken stock,

(page 58 or purchased)

3 tablespoons fresh lime or lemon juice

1 teaspoon sugar

1/2 cup fresh cilantro sprigs

1 Dice chicken finely, mix well with 1 tablespoon of the fish sauce, and set aside.

2 Peel galangal and slice thinly. Rinse lemon grass, remove outer layer, and cut rest into pieces 1 inch long. Rinse chile, remove stem and cut rest into fine rings. Rinse and core tomatoes, and cut into eighths.

3 In a pot, combine coconut milk with stock and heat. Add galangal, lemon grass, chile, remaining fish sauce, citrus juice and sugar. Simmer for 5 minutes.

4 Add diced chicken and tomatoes and simmer gently for another 5 minutes or until chicken is cooked through. Meanwhile, rinse cilantro, shake dry and remove leaves from stems. Salt soup to taste, and garnish servings with cilantro leaves.

Prep time: 25 minutes
Calories per serving: 185

Also good:
Replace half the chicken with small peeled and de-veined shrimp.

63

Shabu Shabu
Japanese fondue

Feeds 4 as a full meal:

1^1/$_3$ lbs. ribeye steak

2 oz. cellophane (mung bean thread) noodles

8 oz. firm tofu

^{1}/$_2$ small Chinese (napa) cabbage

1 cup spinach, rinsed

2 leeks

7 oz. shiitake or oyster mushrooms

2 carrots

Chunk of daikon radish (3-inch section)

About 1 quart dashi stock (page 59 or instant)

For the ponzu sauce:

^{1}/$_3$ cup soy sauce

2 tablespoons fresh lemon juice

3 tablespoons rice wine (sake, mirin)

For the miso sauce:

3 tablespoons sesame seeds

1^1/$_2$ tablespoons light miso

1 tablespoon sugar

^{1}/$_4$ cup rice vinegar

^{1}/$_4$ cup rice wine (sake, mirin)

^{1}/$_4$ cup soy sauce

Hot mustard to taste

^{1}/$_4$ cup dashi stock (page 59 or instant)

1 Freeze beef, wrapped, for 1 hour.

2 Place cellophane noodles in a bowl and cover with hot tap water. Soak for about 5 minutes, then drain in a colander and cut noodles in half using kitchen shears. Cube tofu uniformly.

3 Core napa cabbage and discard any wilted parts; slice into fine strips. Rinse spinach well; discard any tough stems. Remove root end and any wilted parts from leeks; rinse, halve lengthwise and cut into strips ^{1}/$_2$ inch wide by 2 inches long (then rinse again in a colander). Discard mushroom stems; wipe off caps and slice thinly. Peel carrots and slice very thinly on a slight diagonal.

4 Peel daikon and grate finely. Transfer grated daikon to a small bowl and arrange remaining ingredients decoratively on large platters.

5 Remove meat from the freezer and slice thinly with sharp knife. Arrange slices on a platter.

6 For the ponzu sauce: combine soy sauce, lemon juice and rice wine. For the miso sauce: toast sesame seeds in a dry pan briefly until aromatic and a pale golden color. Grind briefly in a food processor, blender, or spice grinder. Stir together with miso, sugar, rice vinegar, rice wine, soy sauce, hot mustard and dashi stock. Transfer sauces to small bowls.

7 Heat dashi stock to a low boil in a pot on the stove, then transfer to an electric or gas burner at the table (or to a fondue pot). Dunk ingredients in the hot stock using chopsticks and cook briefly. Guests can dip cooked items into the sauces provided. The grated daikon is used as a condiment.

Prep time: 45 minutes
(plus 1 hour freezing time)
Calories per serving: 940

Cellophane Noodles with Beef and Mushrooms
Derived from Thai cuisine

Feeds 4 as an appetizer or 2 as a small meal:

6 dried porcini mushrooms, rinsed

3 1/2 oz. cellophane (mung bean thread) noodles

2 fresh red chiles (Fresno=mild, jalapeño=hot, serrano=hotter)

2 shallots

8 fresh chive spears

1/4 lb. oyster or white mushrooms

2 tablespoons fish sauce

1/4 cup fresh lime or lemon juice

1 tablespoon sugar

2 tablespoons oil

1/2 lb. ground beef

1 Place dried porcinis in a bowl, cover with warm water, and soak for about 20 minutes. Soak cellophane noodles in hot water for 10 minutes.

2 Rinse chiles, discard stems (and seeds and ribs for less heat) and cut rest into fine rings. (Always wear gloves when working

with chiles and don't touch your face.) Peel shallots, halve and then cut into strips. Rinse chives, pat dry and cut into 1 1/2-inch lengths. Wipe off oyster or white mushrooms with paper towels, discard stems and slice caps thinly.

3 Drain porcinis and rinse; remove stems and chop caps. Drain cellophane noodles and halve using kitchen shears.

4 Mix fish sauce, citrus juice and sugar. Heat oil in a pan. Sauté porcinis and oyster mushrooms briefly over high heat. Add ground beef and cook, stirring, until it becomes crumbly. Add chiles and shallots; sauté briefly. Stir in noodles and heat through for 1–2 minutes. Add fish sauce mixture and chives, stir well and transfer to a serving bowl. Wait until lukewarm, then stir; salt to taste and enjoy.

Prep time: 20 minutes
(plus 20 minutes soaking time)
Calories per serving (4): 300

Cucumber Salad with Fruit
For an Asian party

Feeds 4 as an appetizer or side dish:

2 tablespoons dried shrimp (Asian grocery)

1 cucumber

1 small pineapple

1 mango

2 shallots

4 cloves garlic

3 fresh red Fresno chile peppers

1 tablespoon oil

1 tablespoon brown sugar

2 teaspoons fish sauce

1/4 cup fresh lime juice

Salt

Cilantro leaves for garnish

1 Mix dried shrimp with 3 1/2 tablespoons warm water; soak for about 30 minutes, then drain.

2 Meanwhile, rinse cucumber, trim ends and cut lengthwise into quarters. Scrape out seeds with a spoon and slice quarters cross-wise, 1/4 inch thick. Peel pineapple and cut into slices, then into small chunks. Peel mango and cut fruit away from pit, then into small chunks. Mix together: cucumber, pineapple and mango.

3 Peel shallots and garlic and mince both. Rinse chiles, discard stems and cut rest into rings. Sauté shallots and garlic in the oil for 2–3 minutes while stirring. Add dried shrimp chiles and sugar; continue sautéing until the sugar dissolves. Purée along with the fish sauce and let cool.

4 Combine puréed sauce with lime juice, season with salt, and fold into cucumber and fruit mixture. Let salad marinate a little, then sprinkle with cilantro leaves and serve.

Prep time: 45 minutes
Delicious with: Seafood and meats
Calories per serving: 150

Vegetables with Thai Dressing
Strength in tranquility—prepare everything ahead of time!

Feeds 4 as a snack:

For the dip:

2 tablespoons dried shrimp

2 cloves garlic

2 shallots

2 fresh red Fresno chile peppers

1/4 cup fresh lime juice

2 tablespoons fish sauce

1 tablespoon brown sugar

For dipping:

1 chunk daikon radish (about 1/2 lb.)

5 green onions

4 stalks celery

1 cucumber

2 carrots

6 spears green asparagus

1 For the dip, rinse shrimp and reconstitute in a little hot water for 30 minutes. Meanwhile, thoroughly rinse all vegetables and peel daikon and carrots. Cut all vegetables into uniform sticks for dipping.

2 Drain shrimp. Peel garlic and shallots and mince along with shrimp. Rinse chiles, discard stems, and cut rest into very fine rings.

3 Combine lime juice, fish sauce, sugar and 1/4 cup water and stir well. Mix in shrimp, garlic, shallots, and chiles; transfer to four small bowls. Serve dip alongside individual portions of the raw vegetable sticks.

Prep time: 40 minutes
Calories per serving: 85

Grapefruit Shrimp Salad
Sweet, spicy hot and fruity

Feeds 4 as an appetizer:

1 pink grapefruit

2–3 shallots

1 small cucumber

4 nice lettuce leaves for garnish

1/2 lb. *cooked* peeled shrimp (small), thawed

1 fresh red Fresno chile pepper

3 tablespoons soy sauce

1 tablespoon rice vinegar

2 tablespoons fresh lime or lemon juice

2 tablespoons honey

1/2 teaspoon chile-garlic sauce (Asian grocery)

Mint or cilantro leaves for sprinkling

1 With a sharp knife, peel grapefruit so that no white membrane remains on the outside. Cut out segments from between the inner membranes. Squeeze any lingering juice out of grapefruit halves and from a few of the segments; collect in a small bowl.

2 Peel shallots and slice thinly. Rinse or peel cucumber, halve lengthwise and scrape out seeds with a spoon. Cut cucumber crosswise into thin slices.

3 Rinse lettuce leaves, shake dry, and arrange on four plates. Top with grapefruit segments, shallots, and cucumber, plus the thawed, cooked shrimp. Rinse chile, discard stem and chop rest. Sprinkle on salads.

4 Combine grapefruit juice, soy sauce, rice vinegar, citrus juice, honey and chile-garlic sauce; drizzle over the salad. Sprinkle with herb leaves.

Prep time: 25 minutes
Calories per serving: 80

Gado Gado
A well-known dish—and not just in Indonesia

Feeds 4 as a full meal or 6 as a side:

4 medium-sized, firm potatoes

1/2 lb. green beans

2 carrots

1/2 head white (green) cabbage

1/3 lb. bean sprouts

Salt

1 small cucumber

3 eggs (optional)

5 oz. tofu

2 onions

1 cup vegetable oil for pan-frying

For the sauce:

1 onion

3 cloves garlic

2 fresh red Fresno chiles or 1/4 teaspoon crushed red pepper flakes

2 tablespoons oil

1 1/3 cups roasted salted peanuts

1 cup coconut milk

1 tablespoon tamarind paste (from a jar) or lemon juice

1/4 cup kecap manis (sweet soy sauce)

Basic Tip

Some people love cold vegetables in a salad, others don't. Those who don't can simply turn this salad into a warm main dish. First make the sauce and keep it warm. Then cook the vegetables and keep them warm in an oven set to about 170°F. Don't fry the onion rings and tofu until the very end and then serve with the vegetables and sauce. In this case, you can omit the hard-boiled eggs and/or cucumber, but the dish goes well with rice.

1 Peel potatoes, rinse, and cut into 1/4-inch-thick slices. Rinse beans and trim ends. Peel carrots and slice into 1/4-inch-thick rounds. Remove outer wilted leaves and core from cabbage; slice rest into fine strips. Rinse and drain bean sprouts.

2 Bring a large amount of salted water to a boil. Cook the prepared ingredients in this water: potatoes=10 minutes, beans=6 minutes, carrots=5 minutes, cabbage=2 minutes and sprouts=1 minute. Drain and rinse vegetables with cold water.

3 Peel cucumber and halve lengthwise. Scrape out seeds with a spoon and slice rest finely crosswise. Hard-boil the eggs for 10–12 minutes; let cool. Cut tofu into thin slices and season with salt. Peel onions and slice finely into rings. Heat oil to 350–375°F (use oil thermometer). You can also tell if oil is ready by lowering the handle of a wooden spoon into it—lots of bubbles should rise to the surface around it. Fry onion slices for about 6 minutes and until golden. Then fry tofu for 3 minutes. Drain both on paper towels.

4 For the sauce, peel onion and garlic and dice. Rinse chiles, discard stems and chop (unless using chile flakes). Sauté onion, garlic and chiles in oil. Add peanuts and coconut milk, stir well and bring to a boil. Season to taste with tamarind paste (or lemon juice) and kecap manis. Purée in a blender and let cool. If the sauce is too thick, thin with a little water.

5 Arrange all vegetables, the sprouts, and the tofu on four plates or on one large platter. Peel eggs, cut into eighths and distribute on top along with the onion rings. Serve sauce on the side.

Prep time: 1 1/2 hours
Delicious with: Shrimp crackers
Calories per serving (4): 680

Beef Salad with Toasted Rice
Uncommonly tasty—
from Thailand

Feeds 4 as a starter:

2 tablespoons short- or medium-grain rice

1 lb. beef tenderloin or ribeye

3 shallots

1 piece ginger (3/4-inch section)

2 cloves garlic

1/4 cup fresh cilantro sprigs

1/4 cup fresh mint sprigs

2 tablespoons oil

3 tablespoons fresh lime juice

2 teaspoons sugar

1 tablespoon fish sauce

1 tablespoon soy sauce

1 Heat a pan or wok on the stove. Toast dry rice over medium heat for about 5 minutes, until golden. Let cool, then process in a blender or food processor into very small pieces.

2 Freeze meat slightly and slice as thinly as possible. Peel shallots and slice into rings. Peel ginger and garlic and mince both. Rinse herbs, shake dry, remove any tough stems

and chop rest finely (reserve a few whole leaves for garnish).

3 Heat oil. Sauté meat over high heat for about 2 minutes while stirring well. Add rice pieces, shallots, ginger, garlic, chopped herbs, lime juice, sugar, fish sauce and soy sauce; bring to a rolling boil. Transfer salad to a bowl and let cool. Sprinkle with herb leaves as a garnish.

Prep time: 25 minutes
(not including cooling time)
Calories per serving: 205

Chicken Salad with Cabbage Strips
Especially for parties

Feeds 4:

3/4 lb. chicken breasts

Salt, freshly ground pepper

1/2 head small white (green) cabbage

1 carrot

1 fresh red Fresno chile pepper

4 green onions

2 teaspoons sugar

1 tablespoon fish sauce

1 tablespoon soy sauce

3 tablespoons fresh lime juice

1 tablespoon rice vinegar

1/2 cup fresh cilantro sprigs

1/4 cup fresh mint sprigs

1 Place chicken in a pot and cover with water. Add salt and pepper and bring to a gentle boil. Cover chicken and cook over low heat for about 10 minutes. Let cool in the water.

2 Remove any wilted leaves and core from cabbage; rinse, halve and cut the rest into very fine strips. Peel carrot and cut length-wise into thin slices, then into strips. Rinse chile, discard stem and chop rest finely. Remove root ends and any wilted parts from green onions; rinse and cut into 1 1/2-inch lengths, then into narrower strips.

3 Combine cabbage, carrot strips, chile, green onion strips, salt and sugar; toss together. Let mixture stand at room temperature for about 15 minutes.

4 Mix fish sauce, soy sauce, lime juice, and rice vinegar. Rinse herbs, shake dry, discard tough stems and chop rest coarsely. Drain chicken and shred into bite-size chunks. Combine vegetable mixture, chicken, sauce mixture and herbs. Salt to taste and serve.

Prep time: 35 minutes
(not including cooling time)
Calories per serving: 165

Squid Salad with Basil
Very spicy, very refreshing and once again from Thailand

Feeds 4 as an appetizer:

1 red onion

3/4 cup fresh basil sprigs

2 cloves garlic

1 piece ginger (1/2-inch section)

2 fresh red Fresno chile peppers

1 stalk lemon grass

1 lb. squid (choose the larger ones, and not the frozen kind)

Salt

2 tablespoons fish sauce

3 tablespoons fresh lime juice

1 teaspoon sugar

1 Peel onion, halve, and slice into half-rounds. Rinse basil briefly, shake dry and remove leaves from stems. Tear leaves into smaller pieces but don't chop.

2 Peel garlic and ginger. Rinse chiles and remove stems. Trim ends from lemongrass and remove outermost layer; finely chop the rest along with the garlic, ginger and chiles.

3 Rinse squid and halve lengthwise. Feel inner sack with your fingers. You will probably find a "bone" (looks like a transparent skewer)—pull or cut this out. Cut squid into pieces 1/2 inch x 2 inches. Bring salted water to a boil. Throw in squid, bring to a boil again and simmer for 1 minute. Remove a little piece of squid and test it. If it isn't tender yet, cook it just a bit longer but no longer than 2 minutes. Rinse and drain under cold water.

4 In the meantime, combine fish sauce, lime juice, and sugar to make a sauce. Mix sauce with lemon grass, garlic, ginger, chiles, onion and basil. Stir in squid. Salt to taste; serve salad at room temperature.

Prep time: 30 minutes
Delicious with: Shrimp crackers
Calories per serving: 110

Also good:
If you don't really care for squid but love fish, prepare this salad with fish. Cut cod, sole or other white fish fillets into bite-size pieces and steam for 5 minutes. Or replace squid with shrimp; boil shrimp for 2 minutes or until opaque throughout and proceed with rest of recipe as directed.

Tip:
When this salad is served in a Thai restaurant it not only tastes superb but also looks it. Using a very sharp knife, Asian chefs score the squid in a diamond pattern. The squid then expands and puffs out to reveal the pattern when cooked and looks like a miniature work of art. Try it yourself sometime and impress your guests!

Rice &

Come on, come on, everything into the wok!

Noodles

How can you go wrong with rice? Or with noodles for that matter? These are the two darlings of the Asian starch world.

And not boring, that's for sure. Rice can be brown, basmati, jasmine, short grain, long grain...it's exhausting just thinking about it. And Asian noodles can take the form of wheat, egg, rice or mung bean thread—the list goes on.

So it's time to grab your cooking chopsticks and stir-fry something in your wok to go with your rice or noodles. These staples are so versatile, almost anything will work!

Finger Exercise No. 3
Carrot Tulips

Mastering this exercise will: 1) increase your dexterity and 2) strengthen your appreciation for uniformity.

1. Peel a carrot that's at least ³/₄ inch in diameter. Toward the thicker end, make a cut at an angle towards the end—but don't cut all the way through—so as to form a petal rounded at the top. A sharp paring or bird's beak knife (shown) works well.

2. Working your way around the carrot, cut three more of these petals in the same way. If everything goes well, a tulip-like blossom will be formed that is still barely attached to the carrot at its center. Sever this connection with the tip of the knife (or by twisting the carrot).

3. Then cut the next tulip from the carrot and then the next, continuing until the entire carrot has been used up and you have a bouquet of tulips (e.g., using basil or spinach for the leaves). These are great for nibbling and can even be cooked in the wok.

Greetings, Aunt Betty,

I never would have thought Thailand could be so cold. Yesterday when we arrived in Chiang Mai, the city was shadowed by ominous clouds. So we immediately took a taxi out into the countryside and after spending the whole time discussing food with the driver, he took us home to to eat with his family. That was really something! We imitated everything they did. First we washed our hands, then we drank some water, and then we all got down on mats around a little table (with me sitting cross-legged while Sarah modestly kneeled). The meal started with an enormous bowl of sticky rice and lots of little bowls filled with all kinds of things. So much food? For guests, always, said the driver. But how did your wife know ... ? No matter—we all made balls of rice with our clean hands (right hands only) and courageously dipped them into the various curiosities. It all tasted fantastic and the strange fruits served afterwards were the best I've ever tasted.

Enthusiastically,

Your nephew, Harry

POST
12.06.2002
Basic Services
5

To:
Aunt Betty
123 Homesick Lane
Des Moines, Iowa
United States

Homemade Asian Basics
Mango Chutney

Some people might prefer to eat it for breakfast on flatbread, because they're so crazy about the sweet, sour and spicy tropical flavor of mango chutney. But it's better known as a condiment with curry and rice dishes as prepared in India. The flavor of chutney made with unripe mangos is particularly authentic:

Peel 2 lbs. firm mangos, cut fruit from pits and dice. (Combine mangos with ½ teaspoon salt and let stand in a colander for 30 minutes.) In a dry pan, toast 1½ teaspoons crushed red pepper flakes (or less if desired) for 1 minute over low heat, then remove and set aside. Peel 3 cloves garlic.

In a pan, toast 1 teaspoon mustard seeds (black seeds if possible—Indian grocery) for at least 1 minute. Add 1 tablespoon oil and garlic; sauté briefly with 1 teaspoon ground turmeric. Pour in ⅓ cup mild fruit vinegar (e.g., cider, raspberry) and ⅓ cup water. Add 1 cup lightly packed brown sugar and the crushed red pepper flakes and simmer gently for 10 minutes. Add mangos and cook gently for 15 minutes, then transfer to jars. Marinate for at least 1 week, refrigerated. Keeps for a couple weeks.

Drinking Asian Style:
Rice Wine

In Asia, a fine Chinese shaoxing or Japanese sake is as important as champagne in the western world. Compared to wine and champagne, rice wine has a licorice-vegetable taste—some claim it is like sherry, while others say it's medicinal. But if you look at the way rice wine is made, it is actually more akin to beer.

The Chinese and Japanese use similar brewing processes. Special types of rice (in Japan, there are over 60 types just for sake) are gently milled and ground, then soaked in water and finally steamed. For Chinese rice wine, other grains are added, most commonly wheat. Yeast bacteria are then added to cause the mixture to ferment. The Japanese especially like to include koji, a special type of mold added during fermentation.

After the water and rice have fermented for no more than 3-5 weeks, the liquid (i.e., the rice wine) is separated out and pasteurized. Then aging takes 6 months for Japanese sake and 1 year or longer for Chinese rice wine, which turns an amber color and tastes spicier and less smoky than its younger Japanese cousin. Sake should be light and clear; discolored sake is considered old. And, despite its longer aging period, even Chinese shaoxing rice wine shouldn't be aged too long. Like beer, it should be consumed when fresh.

If the rice wine is of high quality, you won't need to drink it warm or hot. Depending on the rice, the fineness of the grind, the water and the additives, a distinction is made among five different types, the best of which are served alone like whiskey (or even on the rocks) or in mixed drinks.

Rice wine is very yang and goes especially well with fish because it neutralizes the fishy aroma, especially raw fish used in sushi.

Fried Rice
Global player found almost everywhere in Asia

Ideal for leftover rice, as freshly cooked rice is very moist and disintegrates quickly when stir-fried.

Feeds 4:

2½ cups *cooked* long-grain rice

1 stalk celery

1 carrot

1 red bell pepper

1 medium-sized eggplant (about ½ lb.)

5 oz. fresh oyster mushrooms or ½ cup canned bamboo shoots

2 fresh red Fresno chiles

3–4 shallots

2 cloves garlic

⅓ cup vegetable oil

2 tablespoons rice wine (sake, mirin)

2 tablespoons soy sauce

Salt (if needed)

2 eggs

1 If you don't happen to have any leftover rice, make rice now for stir-frying tomorrow. To do so, combine 1¼ cups rice with 2½ cups water in a pot without salt. Bring to a boil, reduce heat to the lowest level, cover and cook for about 20 minutes. Then let cool, transfer to a bowl and store in the refrigerator. Rice can be used when cooled.

2 Once you have rice from the previous day, rinse vegetables, peel carrots and brush off mushrooms with a paper towel. Slice celery thinly and remove any loose threads. Cut carrot lengthwise into very thin slices and then into thin 2-inch-long sticks. Cut bell pepper into narrow strips. Dice eggplant. Cut mushrooms (or drained bamboo shoots) into strips.

3 Rinse chiles, remove stems and cut into fine rings (always wear gloves when working with hot peppers and don't touch your face). Peel shallots and garlic and slice both thinly.

4 In a wok or large pan, heat half the oil. Stir-fry cooked rice for 2–3 minutes and then remove. Pour remaining oil into wok or pan. First stir-fry garlic, chiles and shallots, then add eggplant and sauté for 1 minute. Next add all the other vegetables and the mushrooms or bamboo shoots and stir-fry for about 3 minutes, stirring constantly so everything cooks evenly.

5 Season to taste with rice wine, soy sauce and, if desired, salt. Stir in rice and heat through. Whisk eggs well in a small bowl and pour over rice and vegetables, stirring rapidly until eggs are no longer liquid, but not so long that the mixture dries out. It's ready!

Prep time: 30 minutes
(with rice from the previous day)
Delicious with: Cucumber Salad with Fruit (page 66), plus with sambal oelek and soy sauce on the table and a cold light beer (or rice wine) to drink
Calories per serving: 355

Basic Tip

When you're making fried rice, you can let yourself go—throw almost anything in the pan with the rice. For example, cooked duck breast strips with oyster mushrooms and Chinese cabbage (in this case, leave out the egg), or any other vegetable you happen to have on hand, or shrimp with bell peppers and peas, or chicken breast with ginger, bamboo shoots and cilantro. Just look in the refrigerator and/or pantry and go for it!

Cooked Rice— Different Every Time

Rice is an appropriate side dish with almost every main dish in this book (see page 16 to find out how to cook it right). It can be very simple (i.e., pure and without frills) but doesn't have to be. Here are a few ideas that can make your rice more elegant:

Saffron Almond Rice

Thoroughly rinse 1⅓ cups basmati rice in a strainer and drain. Stir a couple saffron threads into 3 tablespoons warm water (first crumble threads between your fingers). Melt 1 tablespoon clarified butter or canola oil in a pot and briefly sauté 2 tablespoons sliced almonds, 1 cinnamon stick and 5 green cardamom pods. Then add rice and sauté while stirring constantly. Pour in saffron mixture and about 2½ cups water and bring to a boil. Add salt, cover and cook over very low heat for about 20 minutes. Saffron Almond Rice goes especially well with Indian recipes such as Tandoori Chicken (page 140) and Saffron Fish (page 119).

Turmeric Rice with Shallots

Combine 1⅓ cups long-grain rice, 2 cups water, 1 teaspoon ground turmeric, ½ teaspoon ground coriander, 1 pinch ground cinnamon and salt in a pot. Bring to a boil, cover and cook over very low heat for about 20 minutes. Meanwhile, peel 6 shallots, slice into rings and pan-fry in ¼ cup oil until browned and crispy, but not black. Sprinkle shallot rings on rice. Turmeric rice goes with vegetable dishes, fried tofu and meat or fish dishes that include sauces.

Coconut Rice

Combine 1⅓ cups long-grain jasmine rice, 1 cup coconut milk and 1 cup water in a pot with 2 fresh or frozen kaffir lime leaves and salt; bring to a boil. Cover and cook over very low heat for about 20 minutes. Meanwhile in a dry pan over medium heat, toast 2 tablespoons grated coconut and sprinkle on top of cooked coconut rice. This goes especially well with all spicy dishes, such as curry.

Curried Rice with Chicken
A little excursion to India

Feeds 4:

1⅓ cups basmati rice

1 lb. chicken breasts

2 onions

1 piece ginger (¾-inch section)

1 green bell pepper

2 tomatoes

3 tablespoons clarified butter or ghee, (specialty store, or make your own—heat a stick of butter until melted, then skim the top until no more white solids remain)

1 cinnamon stick

4 whole cloves

4 green cardamom pods

2 teaspoons curry powder (or 1 teaspoon ground turmeric and 1 teaspoon Hungarian hot paprika)

¼ cup yogurt

Salt

2 tablespoons raisins

2 tablespoons sliced almonds

1 Rinse rice using a fine mesh strainer until water runs clear. Drain well. Cut chicken breast into bite-size cubes.

2 Peel onions and dice. Peel ginger and mince or grate. Rinse and halve bell pepper. Remove seeds and ribs, discard stem and dice rest finely. Core tomatoes and place in a bowl; cover with boiling water, let stand briefly, rinse with cold water and slip off peels. Dice the peeled tomatoes.

3 In a pot, heat 1 tablespoon of the clarified butter. Sauté diced chicken well until golden on all sides and remove (this will cook more later). Melt another tablespoon of the butter and sauté the cinnamon stick, cloves, cardamom pods and curry powder for 1 minute.

4 Add onions, ginger and bell pepper; sauté briefly. Add rice and stir to mix well. Stir in tomatoes, yogurt and 2 cups water. Cover and simmer over low heat for about 15 minutes.

5 Add chicken and raisins, and cook for 5 minutes or until the rice is al dente.

6 Meanwhile, melt remaining clarified butter in a small pan. Stir in sliced almonds and sauté until golden. Salt the chicken and rice mixture to taste. Garnish with the toasted almonds.

Prep time: 40 minutes
Delicious with: Yogurt mixed with lots of freshly chopped mint and, if desired,

1 chopped fresh red Fresno chile (mild to medium hot), ground cumin and salt
Calories per serving: 575

Rice with Seafood
A little hot but not as spicy as in Thailand

Feeds 4:

1¼ cups aromatic rice (e.g., jasmine, basmati)

½ lb. squid

Salt

½ lb. raw shrimp

1 onion

4 cloves garlic

5 green onions

2 tomatoes

3 tablespoons oil

1 tablespoon red curry paste

2 tablespoons fish sauce

1 tablespoon fresh lime juice

1 teaspoon brown sugar

1 tablespoon cilantro leaves

1 Rinse aromatic rice and and add with 2 cups water to a pot; bring to a boil. Cover, reduce heat to lowest level and cook for 15–20 minutes. At this point it should be al dente (tender yet firm, and not mushy); all the water should be absorbed. Remove cover and let cool.

2 Meanwhile, rinse squid well and cut into bite-size pieces. Blanch in boiling salted water for 1 minute (don't start counting until the water returns to a boil). Rinse squid well with very cold water. Peel shrimp and see whether there's a dark, narrow stripe down their backs. If so, cut through the first layer of meat along this vein and pull it out. Rinse shrimp and pat dry.

3 Peel onion, halve and cut into strips. Peel and slice garlic. Remove root end and any wilted parts from green onions, rinse rest and cut into 1/4-inch sliced rounds. Rinse tomatoes, remove cores and cut rest into eighths.

4 After rice has cooled, heat oil and sauté onion and garlic for about 1 minute. Stir in curry paste. Add squid and shrimp; sauté for 1 minute. Add rice, tomatoes and green onions. Season with fish sauce, lime juice and sugar and sauté for about another 2 minutes. Sprinkle with cilantro and serve.

Prep time: 40 minutes
Delicious with: Chile sauce (page 57) and Spicy Cucumber Salad (see Tip on page 46)
Calories per serving: 420

Nasi Goreng
National dish of Indonesia and Malaysia

Feeds 4:

1 1/4 cups jasmine rice

1 piece ginger (3/4-inch section)

1 stalk lemon grass

2 cups chicken stock

4 whole cloves

1 teaspoon sambal oelek (Asian grocery)

1/2 teaspoon ground turmeric

1 teaspoon ground cumin

1 pinch ground cinnamon

2 eggs

Salt

3 tablespoons oil

1 red bell pepper

1 green bell pepper

1/3 lb. cooked ham

1/3 lb. small, peeled, *cooked* shrimp

3 tablespoons kecap manis (sweet soy sauce, Asian grocery)

1 Using a fine mesh strainer, rinse rice well and drain.

2 Peel ginger and slice thinly. Rinse lemon grass, remove outer layer, trim ends, and cut rest into 3/4-inch lengths. In a pot, combine: ginger, lemon grass, chicken stock, cloves, sambal oelek, turmeric, cumin and cinnamon. Add rice, bring to a boil, cover, reduce heat and cook for about 20 minutes. (Afterwards, remove lemon grass and cloves.)

3 Meanwhile, whisk eggs and 1–2 tablespoons water thoroughly; salt lightly. In a nonstick pan, heat 1 tablespoon of the oil. Pour in egg mixture, spread around thinly and cook until it sets. Remove from pan and let cool.

4 Rinse and halve bell peppers. Remove seeds and ribs, discard stems and cut rest into narrow strips. Finely dice ham.

5 Heat remaining oil and sauté ham and peppers until pepper strips are crisp-tender. Add ham, peppers, shrimp and kecap manis to rice; stir. Salt to taste. Cut omelet into narrow strips and fold into rice. Cover pan and heat briefly, until egg and shrimp are heated through.

Prep time: 40 minutes
Delicious with: Cucumber Salad with Fruit (page 66); sambal oelek as a condiment; beer or rice wine to drink
Calories per serving: 670

Gyoza
Similar to pot stickers, only boiled

Feeds a crowd:

3½ cups flour, plus more if needed

1 piece ginger (¾-inch section)

1 leek

12 spears fresh chives

¾ lb. lean ground pork

1 tablespoon rice wine (sake, mirin)

2 tablespoons soy sauce

2 teaspoons rice vinegar

1 teaspoon sesame oil

Salt

For the sauce:

⅓ cup rice vinegar

⅓ cup soy sauce

2 teaspoons sesame oil (or more to taste)

1 Mix flour and 1 cup lukewarm water well; then knead into a smooth, soft dough that doesn't stick to your fingers. If it's too soft, knead in a little more flour. If too dry, add a little water. Wrap dough loosely in a damp dishtowel and let stand for 30 minutes.

2 Prepare the filling: Peel ginger and grate or mince. Trim root end and any dark green wilted parts from leek; slit open lengthwise, rinse well and chop very finely. Rinse chives, shake dry and mince.

3 In a bowl, combine ground pork, ginger, leek, chives, rice wine, soy sauce, rice vinegar, sesame oil and salt; mix until well-combined.

4 Divide dough into four pieces and shape each into a cylinder ¾ inch thick. Cut pieces ¾ inch long from the cylinders and roll into balls. Roll out each ball into a very thin round. You should have about 40–60 pieces.

5 Distribute about a half teaspoon of filling on top of each dough round. Fold dough over the top into the shape of crescents (half moons) and press the edges very firmly together.

6 Bring a large pot of lightly salted water to a boil. Throw in a bunch of the gyoza— but don't crowd the pot; return to a boil, then reduce heat to medium and simmer for about 4 minutes. Remove with a slotted spoon. Continue in this way with each batch until finished.

7 For the sauce, mix rice vinegar, soy sauce and sesame oil; transfer to 4 small bowls. Serve sauce alongside gyoza for dipping.

Prep time: 1¼ hours
Delicious followed by: A light soup or a vegetable dish with rice
Calories per serving: 485

Basic Tip

Pot stickers are another type of Asian dumpling— this time Chinese. Buy the "wrappers" frozen or refrigerated from an Asian market. You can then use the same gyoza filling or substitute shrimp for the pork. Pot stickers can be sautéed, deep-fried or cooked in a bamboo steamer. They taste great with a sauce made from rice vinegar, soy sauce and hot chile oil or (not very authentic but very good) with Chile Sauce (page 57). Another tip: you can cut this recipe in half for feeding a smaller crowd (but still makes a lot).

Chile-Garlic Noodles and Chicken
Spicy and Easy

Feeds 4:

8 oz. vermicelli-sized Chinese egg noodles

2 stalks lemon grass

4 fresh red Fresno chile peppers

2 cloves garlic

1 shallot

1 piece ginger (¾-inch section)

⅓ lb. chicken breast

2 tablespoons soy sauce

8 oz. spinach

⅓ lb. bean sprouts

1 small cucumber

⅓ cup oil

Salt

Crushed red pepper flakes to taste

Mint and/or basil leaves for sprinkling

1 Add noodles to a large pot of boiling, salted water. Immediately remove pot from heat and let noodles soak for 4 minutes. Then drain and rinse well under cold water.

2 Rinse lemon grass, trim ends, remove outer later, and chop rest finely. Rinse chiles, remove stems, and mince rest finely. Peel and mince garlic, shallot, and ginger. Mix all of these together and mince even finer to create a seasoning paste.

3 Cut chicken into thin strips and mix with soy sauce. Rinse spinach well, drain, discard any thick stems and tear any large leaves into smaller pieces. Rinse and drain bean sprouts. Rinse cucumber, halve lengthwise, scrape out seeds with a spoon, and slice rest thinly crosswise.

4 Heat oil in a nonstick pan. Stir-fry noodles briefly, then remove. Add chicken and bean sprouts; stir. Add cucumber and cook briefly. Stir in seasoning paste mixture and sauté for 1 minute. Add spinach, and stir, cooking until it wilts. Then add noodles; salt to taste. If you desire more heat, add crushed red pepper flakes to taste. Sprinkle with fresh mint and/or basil leaves, and serve.

Prep time: 40 minutes
Delicious preceded by: Grapefruit Shrimp Salad (page 67)
Calories per serving: 380

Stir-Fried Beef and Rice Noodles
Wide like Italian tagliatelle but authentically Thai

Feeds 4:

8 oz. wide rice noodles

1 lb. beef tenderloin, filet or ribeye

1 lb. bok choy (2 medium heads; or substitute broccoli)

2 onions

4 cloves garlic

⅓ cup vegetable oil

3 tablespoons oyster sauce

1 tablespoon fish sauce

1 tablespoon sugar

Salt (if needed)

For sprinkling:

⅔ cup roasted salted peanuts, chopped

Chili powder

Rice vinegar

Cilantro leaves

1 Cook noodles in boiling water for about 4 minutes; rinse and drain.

2 Against the grain, slice beef thinly and then cut into wide strips. Rinse bok choy, halve lengthwise and then cut crosswise into wide strips. Pre-cook bok choy in boiling, salted water for 2 minutes, then remove and drain. Peel onions, halve and then cut into wide strips. Peel garlic and slice thinly.

3 Heat oil in a wok or large pan and sauté garlic, onions, and beef for about 2 minutes. Add bok choy and sauté another 2 minutes.

4 Add noodles, oyster sauce, fish sauce and sugar; heat thoroughly while stirring constantly. Salt to taste.

5 Serve with the following alongside as condiments (guests can pick and choose): peanuts, chili powder, rice vinegar and cilantro.

Prep time: 30 minutes
Calories per serving: 635

Crispy Noodles with Pork and Vegetables
Wok magic

Feeds 4:
½ lb. ground pork
2 tablespoons rice wine (sake, mirin)
2 stalks celery
1 small red bell pepper
1 carrot
1 piece ginger (¾-inch section)
4 cloves garlic
2 tablespoons oil plus 3 cups for deep-frying, (peanut, vegetable or canola)
2 tablespoons black bean sauce, (Asian grocery)
¼ cup soy sauce
5 oz. cellophane noodles (mung bean thread type)

1 Mix ground pork with rice wine; let stand. Rinse celery and bell pepper. Peel carrot. Halve bell pepper and discard stem, seeds, and ribs. Then dice celery, pepper and carrot finely. Peel ginger and garlic; mince both.

2 Heat oil in a wok or pan and sauté ginger and garlic. Add vegetables and stir-fry for 2 minutes. Then add pork and cook until crumbly—break apart the meat while stirring.

3 Next add black bean sauce, soy sauce and ½ cup water; stir, bring to a low boil and then reduce heat to very low (keep hot).

4 Heat oil for frying; to test, insert a wooden spoon handle into the oil. When a lot of bubbles congregate around it, it's hot enough. (Or use an oil thermometer; should be 350–375°F.) Divide the cellophane noodles into two or three portions, untangle them a little and drop them into the oil one batch at a time. When the noodles puff up and turn snow-white, remove from oil with a metal slotted spoon and drain on a paper towel-lined plate. After the last batch, transfer fried noodles to individual bowls, cover with meat sauce, and serve immediately.

Prep time: 25 minutes
Delicious preceded by: Tomato Egg Flower Soup (page 61) or Chicken Salad with Cabbage Strips (page 70)
Calories per serving: 340

Rice Noodles with Spicy Pork
Vietnamese seduction

Feeds 4:

1½ lbs. pork loin chop/roast or tenderloin

⅓ cup sugar

2 tablespoons fish sauce

8 oz. thin rice noodles

6 green onions

¾ cup fresh mint sprigs

¾ cup fresh basil sprigs

¾ cup fresh cilantro sprigs

1 cucumber

½ lb. bean sprouts

⅔ cup roasted salted peanuts, chopped

2 tablespoons oil

For the sauce:

2 fresh red Fresno chiles (mild to medium hot)

2 cloves garlic

3 tablespoons soy sauce

2 tablespoons fish sauce

3 tablespoons fresh lime juice

1 Cut pork into bite-size strips. Melt sugar in a pot while stirring until golden. Add fish sauce and bring to a rapid boil. Mix this sauce with uncooked pork strips; marinate. Place rice noodles in a bowl, cover with warm water and soak for 20 minutes.

2 Remove root ends and any dark green or wilted parts from green onions, rinse and slice thinly into rings. Rinse herbs, shake dry and discard any tough stems. Rinse cucumber, halve lengthwise, remove seeds with a spoon and cut into narrow strips. Cook bean sprouts in salted, boiling water for 1 minute, then drain. Divide green onions, cucumber, bean sprouts and peanuts among four dinner plates (for serving).

3 For the dip, rinse chiles, discard stems and chop rest finely (wear gloves and don't touch your face). Peel garlic and mince. Mix chiles, garlic, soy sauce, fish sauce and lime juice; transfer to four individual bowls. Drain noodles and distribute on the dinner plates. Serve sauce alongside.

4 Heat oil in a wok or pan and sauté pork over high heat in 2 batches for about 2 minutes each. When the second batch is done, return the first batch to the pan and heat. Distribute meat near the noodles on the plates. Guests can mix ingredients together and enjoy.

Prep time: 40 minutes
Delicious preceded by: Spicy-Sour Shrimp Soup (page 60) or Squid Salad with Basil (page 71)
Calories per serving: 760

Curried Noodles with Coconut Milk
A little sweet, a little spicy, a little yellow

Feeds 4:

1 piece ginger (¾-inch section)

4 cloves garlic

2 stalks lemon grass

2 teaspoons sambal oelek

1 teaspoon ground turmeric

1 teaspoon ground coriander seed

1 teaspoon ground cumin

Salt

8 oz. thin Chinese egg noodles

1 leek

¼ lb. fresh oyster mushrooms

1 red bell pepper

8 oz. tofu

2 cups oil for deep-frying and sautéing

1⅔ cups canned coconut milk

2−3 tablespoons kecap manis
(sweet soy sauce)

1 Peel ginger and garlic and chop both finely. Rinse lemon grass, trim ends, remove

outer layer, chop coarsely and process along with ginger and garlic in a food processor. (Or, chop finely, or use a mortar and pestle.) Mix this paste with sambal oelek, turmeric, coriander, cumin and salt.

2 Cook noodles in boiling water for 3–5 minutes or until cooked through. Drain and rinse under cold water. Remove root end and any dark green or wilted parts from leek, slit open lengthwise and rinse thoroughly. Cut into 2-inch lengths, then into narrow strips. Wipe off mushrooms with paper towels, discard stems and slice caps. Rinse bell pepper, halve, discard interior and stem and cut rest into strips.

3 Cut tofu into 1/2-inch cubes. Heat oil in a wok or pan to 350–375°F (use an oil thermometer). Pat tofu dry with paper towels, deep-fry in hot oil until golden, then remove with a metal slotted utensil. Pour oil out of the wok or pan (into another pan until cooled; then oil can be place in a container for later use), leaving only a thin coating.

4 Sauté seasoning paste mixture in pan for 2 minutes. Add leek, bell pepper and mushrooms; sauté for 3–4 minutes. Pour in coconut milk and bring to a low boil. Stir in noodles and tofu; heat through. Add kecap manis and salt to taste, then serve.

Prep time: 40 minutes
Delicious preceded by: Cucumber Salad with Fruit (page 66)
Calories per serving: 385

Udon Noodles with Daikon
Almost a soup but always a main dish in Japan

Feeds 4:

1 leek

4 shiitake mushrooms (may substitute 8 large white or brown cremini mushrooms)

1/3 lb. daikon radish

4–8 pieces surimi (kamaboko, imitation crab), or 4 oz. tofu

14 oz. dry udon noodles

3 cups dashi stock (page 59 or instant dashi; or vegetable or chicken stock mixed with equal parts water)

1/2 cup soy sauce

1 tablespoon rice wine (sake, mirin)

1 teaspoon sugar

Red radishes for garnishing

For serving:

Wasabi (from a tube) and, if desired, Japanese pickled ginger

1 Remove root end and any dark green or wilted parts from leek, slit open lengthwise, rinse and cut into strips 1/4 inch wide. Wipe off shiitake mushrooms with paper towels, discard stems and cut caps into strips. Peel daikon, cut into very thin slices, and then into strips about 1/2 inch wide. Cut surimi or tofu diagonally into thin slices.

2 Cook noodles in boiling water for about 10 minutes. But don't let them get too soft! Test a noodle after 8 minutes.

3 Bring dashi stock to a boil with soy sauce, mirin and sugar. Add leek and cook for 2 minutes. Add mushrooms and daikon and cook another 2 minutes. Then add noodles and heat. Top with surimi or tofu, then with slices of red radish to garnish; ready to serve. If desired, serve wasabi and pickled ginger at the table as accompaniments.

Prep time: 25 minutes
Delicious preceded by: Spinach with Sesame Sauce (page 97)
Calories per serving: 635

Vegetab

Asia knows how to be Italian...

les

Here's an interesting theory for you: Italian and Asian cuisine are often a lot alike. Both are rural cuisines that developed out of necessity. Both bring out everything an ingredient has to offer, and both gladly incorporate foreign influences into their menu— seamlessly—as if they'd thought it up themselves. Both love rice and noodles, and both do a lot with vegetables but don't much care for vegetables as side dishes.

That's why one favorite Asian main dish is wok-cooked vegetables. It can take a different form every day, just as pasta is served different ways each day in Italy. And this is a good thing, because the many vegetarians on the Asian continent love variety. And they love tofu, Asia's most famous vegetable-based food. Some Americans see tofu as bland, but we see it a little differently. Just try the recipe on page 102 and you'll see what we mean.

Finger Exercise No. 4
Tomato Blossoms

As you master this exercise, you will learn that we must sometimes join together if we are to realize our full potential.

1. For every blossom you wish to make, find three cherry tomatoes of varying sizes. Make two cuts through each one in a criss-cross pattern so that the quarters still hold together.

2. Then remove the seedy flesh, carefully but thoroughly, and stack the tomatoes one inside another.

3. Cut a suitable-sized cube of tofu (or white daikon radish) and set it inside the innermost tomato so that it opens slightly. That's it.

Hi Aunt Betty,

What a relaxing place Asia would be if the Europeans hadn't introduced them to chile peppers from America! Don't misunderstand me, I have nothing against the joys of any particular continent, but was that absolutely necessary? I mean, I've been in India for 3 days now and I have no taste buds left. I asked Eric (the guy I met on the plane who wants to go to Madras with me) what the point was. He says it's good for you because the spiciness opens your pores, makes you sweat and cools you off. Yes, on top of everything else, it's hot outside! Sure, he then gives me the story about tea, how it's much better to drink hot drinks when you're hot. And milk helps cut the spiciness. So is that it, I ask him? We don't taste anything, we just sit here and sweat and don't even get to drink beer? And what do you think Eric says? That I should hold on for just 3 more days and everything'll be okay—for now I should just relax. It does seem like things are getting a little better.

Let's hope so!

Your nephew, Frank

To:
Aunt Betty
123 Homesick Lane
Des Moines, Iowa
United States

12.06.2002
POST
Basic Services
5

Homemade Asian Basics
Sambal

Some say a "real man" is someone who can swallow a teaspoonful of wasabi without hesitating. But back when soy sauce was still considered to be exotic, the same rite of passage existed using sambal oelek, the Southeast Asian paste made of so many chiles that no Asian man would dare eat it by the spoonful. This spicy condiment has a milder cousin, sambal bajak, a cooked version that's best served with rice and stir-fried meats.

For sambal oelek: Roast ½ lb. red chiles (⅓ of which are very hot, e.g., Thailand's bird's eye chiles and ⅔ that are milder such as fresh red Fresno chiles) in a 425° oven until they turn a little brown. Let cool, clean, chop and crush in a mortar or food processor along with 2 tablespoons brown sugar. Mix with 2 tablespoons canola or peanut oil, 3 tablespoons fresh lemon juice and 2 tablespoons fish sauce.

For sambal bajak: Peel 1 piece ginger (½-inch section), 3 cloves garlic and 1 onion. Rinse and remove the outer layer of 1 stalk lemon grass and rinse 10 fresh red Fresno chiles (discard stems, seeds and ribs). Chop all ingredients coarsely. In a pan, sauté 1 tablespoon shrimp paste (made of dried shrimp—available in Asian markets) for about 5 minutes. Then add to blender with all previous ingredients, together with 1 tablespoon peanut butter and ¼ cup oil; pulse to combine coarsely. Place back in the pan and sauté mixture on low for 10 minutes. Then add 2 tablespoons tamarind paste, 2 tablespoons water and 2 tablespoons brown sugar; simmer for 20–30 minutes while stirring periodically.

Refrigerated and tightly sealed in jars, sambals keep for weeks.

Drinking Asian Style:
Milk

Yes, we're talking about that white stuff from cows containing milk sugar (called lactose) for which many Asians have a low tolerance. Actually there's a growing number of Asians in Japan and the continent's larger, westernized cities such as Shanghai, Hong Kong and Singapore who are having fewer problems with milk. Why is this? Maybe it's because delicious milk-based teas and coffees have become so popular, people are finding they can tolerate milk after all? And in Southeast Asia where they like their coffee strong, they like it even better with a shot of sweetened condensed milk.

And then, of course, there's India where milk is the only thing people are allowed to take from the sacred cow, a practical necessity for visitors whose mouths are burning up with spices—especially after eating a curry. This is particularly true of lassi, a drink containing milk or yogurt which ranges from salty and spicy to sweet and fruity. A mango lassi can be a lifesaver in an emergency!

Yogurt is also very important in Indian cuisine. In marinades, it makes the Tandoori Chicken tender, or it's served in cooling sauces that tame the fiery taste of curries.

Wok Vegetables
Something for everyone

Feeds 4 or 6 if served with something else:

2 cloves garlic

2–3 shallots

1 piece ginger ($\frac{1}{2}$-inch section)

1 stalk lemon grass

1 fresh red Fresno chile pepper

1 leek

1 lb. green asparagus

$\frac{1}{4}$ cup oil

$\frac{1}{4}$ cup soy sauce

2 tablespoons rice wine (sake, mirin)

1 teaspoon sugar

Salt (if needed)

Cilantro leaves for sprinkling

1 Peel garlic and shallots and slice thinly. Peel ginger and mince or grate. Rinse lemon grass, trim ends, remove outer layer and chop rest. Rinse chile, discard stem and slice rest thinly into rings.

2 Remove roots and any dark green or wilted parts from leek, slit open lengthwise, rinse very well and cut into narrow strips. Rinse asparagus, trim ends, cut into $\frac{3}{4}$-inch lengths; set aside tips.

3 Heat oil in a wok or pan; sauté garlic, shallots, ginger, lemon grass and chile. Add asparagus (without tips) and stir-fry for 2 minutes. Stir constantly!

4 Add asparagus tips and leek and continue stir-frying for 2 more minutes. Mix together soy sauce, rice wine and sugar and add. Salt to taste, sprinkle with cilantro and serve.

Prep time: 30 minutes
Delicious with: Rice or noodles
such as soba or udon
Calories per serving (6): 90

More Wok Vegetables

Green Beans with Shiitake Mushrooms and Garlic

If shiitakes are the dried type, soak 8 in luke-warm water for about 20 minutes (otherwise, just brush off 8 fresh ones with a paper towel). Clean 1 lb. green beans, rinse and cut each in half; cook in boiling, salted water for 4 minutes. Drain mushrooms (if soaked), discard stems and slice caps. Peel 8 cloves garlic and slice. Heat $\frac{1}{4}$ cup oil in a wok or pan and sauté beans and mushrooms, stir-frying for 4 minutes. Test the beans to see whether they're crisp-tender. If not, stir-fry a little longer. Add garlic and stir-fry for 1 minute. Add about $\frac{1}{4}$ cup soy sauce, 1 table-spoon sesame oil and hot chile oil to taste.

Spicy White Cabbage

Rinse 1$\frac{1}{4}$ lbs. white (green) cabbage, remove core and slice rest into $\frac{1}{4}$-inch strips. Crumble 2 dried chiles (wear gloves and don't touch your face). Heat $\frac{1}{4}$ cup oil in a wok or pan and sauté cabbage strips with chiles for 3–4 minutes. Salt to taste and serve. Or season with a sweet and sour sauce: Combine $\frac{1}{4}$ cup rice vinegar and 2 tablespoons sugar and add. For a Japanese version: mix $\frac{1}{4}$ cup rice vinegar and $\frac{1}{4}$ cup sugar—add and drizzle with sesame oil before serving.

Spicy Bean Sprouts with Coconut

Rinse 1 lb. bean sprouts and drain in a colander. (Or use only $\frac{3}{4}$ lb. bean sprouts plus 1 small red bell pepper cut in strips.) Peel 4 shallots, halve each lengthwise, and cut into strips. Heat $\frac{1}{4}$ cup oil in a wok or

pan and sauté shallots with $\frac{1}{2}$ to 1 teaspoon crushed red pepper flakes. Add bean sprouts and 1 cup grated unsweetened coconut; stir-fry for 2–3 minutes. Add salt and up to 2 tablespoons fresh lime juice, to your taste.

Vegetables with Oyster Sauce

Rinse $\frac{1}{2}$ lb. broccoli florets and blanch in boiling, salted water for 2–3 minutes. Rinse $\frac{3}{4}$ lb. white (green) cabbage, discard core, and cut rest into strips. Rinse 1 leek, slit open lengthwise, rinse very well and slice crosswise thinly. Peel 4 garlic cloves and slice. Heat 3 tablespoons oil in a wok or pan and stir-fry all the vegetables along with the garlic for 3–4 minutes. Pour in 6 tablespoons oyster sauce, stir-fry briefly, and serve.

Greens with Oyster Mushrooms

Wipe off $\frac{1}{4}$ lb. oyster mushrooms with a paper towel; cut into strips. Rinse a small head of romaine, discard core, and cut rest into strips (or use an equivalent amount of bok choy, spinach or other green). Peel 1 piece ginger ($\frac{1}{2}$-inch section), 3 cloves garlic and 3 shallots; chop all three finely. Heat 2 tablespoons oil in a wok or pan and sauté ginger, garlic and shallots. Stir-fry mushrooms briefly, then add greens. Combine 2 table-spoons black bean sauce, 2 tablespoons rice wine (sake, mirin), 2 tablespoons soy sauce, 1 teaspoon sugar and $\frac{1}{3}$ cup water and add. Stir 1 teaspoon cornstarch into $\frac{1}{2}$ tablespoon cold water, mix in with vegetables and bring briefly to a boil; serve at once, preferably with rice.

Bok Choy and Bell Peppers with Kaffir Lime Leaves

Rinse 2 stalks bok choy (about 1 lb.), discard tough base, and cut leaves lengthwise into eighths and then halve these. Rinse 1 red bell pepper, discard stem and contents, and cut rest into strips. Rinse 2 red Fresno chiles, remove stems and cut rest into rings. Rinse 2 stalks lemon grass (trim ends and remove outer layer) and cut into $\frac{1}{2}$-inch sections. Peel 2 cloves garlic and slice. Mince 4 fresh or frozen kaffir lime leaves as finely as possible. Sauté chiles, lemon grass, garlic and lime leaves in 2 tablespoons oil. Add bok choy and bell pepper and stir-fry for 4–5 minutes. Season to taste with 2 tablespoons fish sauce and 2 tablespoons fresh lime juice; sprinkle with mint leaves. Before serving, remove lemon grass. Enjoy!

Sweet Potato Curry
Vegetarian-friendly

Feeds 4:

2 sweet potatoes (about 1⅓ lbs.)

1 leek

1 tablespoon oil

1 tablespoon green curry paste

1⅔ cups canned coconut milk

½ lb. cherry tomatoes

1 tablespoon fresh lime juice

Salt

Cilantro leaves for garnish

1 Peel sweet potatoes just like regular potatoes and cut into ¾-inch cubes. Remove root end and any dark green or wilted parts from leek, slit open lengthwise, rinse thoroughly and cut into crosswise strips about ¼ inch wide.

2 Heat oil in a wok or pan. Stir in curry paste and sauté for 1 minute. Add coconut milk, bring to a gentle boil, cooking for 1 minute. Next add sweet potatoes and leek. Cover and simmer over medium heat for about 8 minutes (or until crisp-tender), checking periodically to see if there's enough liquid in the wok or pan. If not, add a little water.

3 Rinse tomatoes and halve. Add along with lime juice to curry and simmer for another 1–2 minutes. Salt to taste and sprinkle with cilantro leaves.

Prep time: 25 minutes
Delicious with: Any kind of rice
Calories per serving: 195

Vegetables and Tofu in Coconut Milk
Even tofu-haters will like this one!

Feeds 4:

8 oz. firm tofu

1 medium-sized eggplant

½ lb. baby spinach

1 red bell pepper

¼ lb. white (green) or Chinese (napa) cabbage

½ lb. snow peas

¼ lb. bean sprouts

3 shallots

1 piece ginger (¾-inch section)

2 cloves garlic

1⅔ cups vegetable oil for deep-frying, and frying

1⅔ cups canned coconut milk

1 teaspoon ground coriander

Salt

1 Cut tofu into ¼-inch-thick strips. Pat dry with paper towels (so they won't splatter in the hot oil).

2 Rinse all vegetables. Cut eggplant into ¾-inch cubes. Sort spinach leaves. Cut bell pepper and cabbage into narrow strips. Leave snow peas whole but trim off ends. Rinse bean sprouts and drain. Peel shallots, ginger and garlic and chop those three finely.

3 Heat oil until very hot in a wok or pan. Lower a wooden spoon handle into the oil. When tiny bubbles appear around it, the oil is hot enough (or use an oil thermometer—should register 350–375°F). Place tofu in the oil using a metal slotted utensil and deep-fry for about 4 minutes, and until golden. Cover a plate with a thick layer of paper towels. Remove tofu from the oil with the slotted utensil and drain on paper towels.

4 Pour oil out of the wok or pan (into another pan—after cooled, seal in a container for future use), leaving only a thin coating.

5 Start by sautéing the eggplant in the oil, then add the snow peas, cabbage and bell pepper, cooking for 2 minutes. Stir in ginger, garlic and shallots; add bean sprouts. After another minute or two, add coconut milk and ground coriander; simmer uncovered for about 5 minutes. Stir in tofu and baby spinach; heat until spinach wilts. Salt to taste.

Prep time: 1 hour
Delicious with: Rice, or thin rice noodles seasoned with soy sauce
Calories per serving: 230

Pumpkin in Tamarind Sauce
Sweet and sour combo

Feeds 4:

2 tablespoons Tamarind paste, (Asian grocery)

2 tablespoons brown sugar

2 tablespoons fish sauce

1 cooking pumpkin or kabocha (about 1³/₄ lbs., yields 1¹/₄ lbs. after cleaning)

6 cloves garlic

10 green onions

¹/₄ cup oil plus more as needed

1 tablespoon fresh lime or lemon juice

Sambal oelek (optional, homemade or from an Asian grocery)

Salt

Cilantro and mint leaves for sprinkling

1 Mix tamarind paste with brown sugar and fish sauce; heat in a small saucepan until the sugar dissolves.

2 Peel pumpkin, halve, remove seeds and loose fibers and cut into ¹/₂-inch cubes.

3 Peel garlic and mince. Remove roots and any dark green or wilted parts from green onions and rinse rest. Set aside some of the green parts for garnishing later and chop the rest finely.

4 Heat 1 tablespoon of the oil in a wok or large pan and sauté garlic and green onions for a couple minutes. Remove garlic and green onions and add to tamarind mixture.

5 Stir-fry pumpkin in remaining oil (you may have to use a little more) for about 5 minutes until the pieces are crisp-tender. Pour tamarind sauce over the top, season to taste with the fresh citrus juice, sambal oelek and salt and simmer for another 5 minutes.

6 Slice the reserved green onions into fine rings and sprinkle over pumpkin dish along with herb leaves.

Prep time: 30 minutes
Delicious with: Any kind of rice
Calories per serving: 190

Tip:

Tamarind has a unique sour taste, particularly suited to the sweet taste of pumpkin. If you find you didn't have enough tamarind paste, or if you'd like this dish to be even more sour, simply add more citrus juice.

Lentil Balls
with Coconut
Chutney
Start the night before

Feeds 4:

For the balls:

1¼ cup dry red lentils

2 fresh red Fresno chiles

1 onion

2 cloves garlic

1 stalk lemon grass

1 teaspoon fennel seeds

Salt

1 tablespoon flour

1 teaspoon baking powder

4 cups oil for deep-frying

For the chutney:

½ cup fresh cilantro sprigs

1 small onion or shallot

⅔ cup yogurt

1 cup grated unsweetened coconut

1 tablespoon sesame oil

2 teaspoons black sesame seeds

Salt

½ teaspoon chili powder

1 For the lentil balls, cover the lentils with water in a bowl and soak overnight.

2 On the next day, drain lentils. Rinse chiles, discard stems and chop rest coarsely. Peel onion and garlic and chop both coarsely. Rinse lemon grass, trim ends, discard outer layer and chop remaining stalk coarsely.

3 Finely purée drained lentils, chiles, onion, garlic and lemon grass in a blender or food processor. Add fennel seeds, salt, flour and baking powder and process to combine. Remove and knead briefly into a dough. Form into walnut-sized balls, moistening your hands as needed.

4 For the chutney, rinse cilantro, shake dry and discard stems; chop rest. Peel onion or shallot and chop. Put these ingredients in a blender along with yogurt and grated coconut; blend to a purée. If it seems too dry, add a little hot water. Combine chutney and sesame oil in a small bowl.

5 In a pan, toast sesame seeds over medium heat in a dry pan until they give off a fine aroma or until they start to pop a bit. Stir them into the chutney. Also add chili powder and salt chutney to taste; refrigerate.

6 In a deep pot, heat frying oil until very hot (an oil thermometer should register 350–375°F). Cover a platter with a thick layer of paper towels. Deep-fry lentil balls in the hot oil a few at a time until golden brown, remove with a slotted metal utensil and let drain on the paper towels. Serve the finished batches alongside chutney.

Prep time: 50 minutes
(plus overnight soaking)
Delicious with: Chapatis (see Tip below)
or any Indian bread
Calories per serving: 660

Basic Tip: Indian Chapati

If you want authentic Indian, serve dishes along-side chapatis (skillet flatbreads). You can either purchase it in Indian markets or make it yourself: Mix and then knead together very thoroughly 1¼ cups cups flour, ½ cup whole wheat flour, 1 teaspoon salt, ½ cup lukewarm water and 1 table-spoon clarified butter or ghee (purchase at an Indian grocery or make yourself by melting and heating butter and skimming off & discarding the white solids). Wrap in a lightly damp towel and let stand for 30 minutes. Then roll out the dough into 8 thin pancakes and fry on medium-high in an ungreased non-stick pan for 1-2 minutes on each side. You can keep the finished chapatis (and lentil balls) warm in a 200°F oven.

Sweet and Sour Asian Potatoes
The Chinese way to economize

Feeds 4:

1 red bell pepper

1 leek

1¼ lb. firm potatoes (red or yukon gold)

⅓ cup oil

2 teaspoons Sichuan peppercorns, (Chinese grocery)

½ cup rice vinegar

2 tablespoons sugar

¼ cup soy sauce

Salt (if needed)

12 fresh chive spears

1 Rinse bell pepper, halve lengthwise and discard stem and interior. Halve again lengthwise and then slice crosswise into narrow strips.

2 Remove roots and any dark green or wilted parts from leek, slit open lengthwise, bend leaves apart and rinse thoroughly; cut into narrow strips. Peel potatoes and cut into thin slices, then into narrow strips. Rinse under cold water in a colander to rinse off some of the starch; drain well on a paper towel-lined plate.

3 Heat oil and Sichuan peppercorns in a wok or large pan. Sauté peppercorns for about 1 minute to infuse the oil, then remove with a slotted utensil and discard.

4 Stir potatoes into the infused oil and stir-fry over medium heat for about 6 minutes until crisp-tender. Add leek and bell peppers and stir-fry for another 2–3 minutes.

5 Stir together rice vinegar, sugar and soy sauce and pour over the potato mixture. Sauté for another 2 minutes. Salt to taste. Rinse chives, shake dry, cut into 1-inch lengths and sprinkle over potatoes.

Prep time: 35 minutes
Delicious with: Other delicate vegetable dishes, e.g., Green Beans with Shiitake Mushrooms and Garlic (page 91) or poultry dishes, e.g., Teriyaki Duck (page 143)
Calories per serving: 245

Sichuan Vegetables
Pickle and enjoy again and again

In China, Sichuan-pickled vegetables are often served as an appetizer but also accompany heavier dishes to aid digestion. And since they keep for a long time (if immersed in pickling liquid, at least 4 months), they're always ready for use. So prepare them and they'll always be ready for you!

Makes enough for about 10 meals:

4½ lbs. vegetables (e.g., white [green] or Chinese [napa] cabbage, daikon, carrots, leek, celery and bell peppers)

1 piece ginger (1½-inch section)

⅔ cup salt

½ cup brown sugar

2 teaspoons crushed red pepper flakes, (or to taste)

6 star anise

2 teaspoons Sichuan peppercorns

½ cup rice wine (sake, mirin)

1 Depending on the type, rinse or peel vegetables, remove all wilted parts, stems and ends, and cut away anything that won't be eaten. Cut vegetables into cubes, slices or sticks, just so they're bite-size. Peel ginger and slice thinly. Transfer vegetables and ginger slices to sterilized jars with screw tops.

2 In a pot, combine salt, sugar, and 2½ quarts water. Throw in pepper flakes, star anise and Sichuan peppercorns and bring to a boil. Stir until the sugar and salt have dissolved.

3 Pour in rice wine, heat through and pour mixture over the vegetables in the jars. The liquid must cover the vegetables completely. If necessary, add boiling water. Seal jars and marinate vegetables for at least 2 days, refrigerated, before serving.

Prep time: 30 minutes
(plus 2 days minimum pickling time)
Delicious with: All meat, poultry and fish dishes—can also be an appetizer
Calories per serving: 60

Spinach with Sesame Sauce
Japanese inspiration

Feeds 4 as a side dish or appetizer:

1 lb. spinach

Salt

2 tablespoons sesame seeds

1 tablespoon light miso (Japanese or specialty grocery)

1 tablespoon soy sauce

1 tablespoon mirin (sweet Japanese rice wine)

2 teaspoons sugar

1 Sort spinach, discarding wilted leaves and thick stems. Fill sink with cold water and swish the spinach around in it. Change water and keep repeating this process until spinach is thoroughly rinsed; then drain spinach in a colander.

2 In a large pot, bring salted water to a boil. Add spinach, cover and cook at a rapid boil for 2–3 minutes. Drain and rinse well under cold water.

3 For the sauce, toast the sesame seeds briefly in a dry pan but be careful—at some point the seeds start to pop and jump! If they do, simply cover and wait until they stop. Pour sesame seeds (which should be a pale golden color and aromatic) into a mortar and crush very finely—or grind the seeds in a spice mill or extra coffee grinder dedicated to spices.

4 Stir together miso, soy sauce and mirin. Add ground sesame seeds and sugar. Transfer spinach to individual bowls; pour sauce over the top and serve chilled.

Prep time: 35 minutes
Delicious with and followed by: Sushi (pages 52–53), Miso Soup (page 60) and Yakitori Skewers (page 129)
Calories per serving: 70

Tip:

You don't have to use spinach. This sauce is also delicious with Swiss chard. In this case, trim off stems and gently simmer leaves in salted water for about 5 minutes. After rinsing under cold water and draining, cut into strips and top with the sesame sauce.

Corn Fritters and Cucumber Spinach Salad
Impressive and not at all difficult

Feeds 4:

For the salad:

1 cucumber

1 lb. fresh spinach

Salt

2 tablespoons roasted salted peanuts

2 fresh red Fresno chiles

2 tablespoons fresh lime juice

1 teaspoon sugar

2 teaspoons sesame oil

For the fritters:

2½ cups canned corn

5 green onions

2 fresh red Fresno chiles

1 piece ginger (½-inch section)

4 sprigs fresh cilantro

3 eggs

2 tablespoons flour

Salt

¼ cup oil

1 For the salad: Rinse cucumber and peel partially—lengthwise in a striped pattern. Then slice crosswise thinly.

2 Sort spinach, discarding wilted leaves and removing any thick stems. Rinse several times in cold standing water in a clean sink or large bowl. Throw spinach in a pot containing a little boiling, salted water, cover and simmer for 2 minutes or until leaves wilt. Then drain, rinsing under very cold water.

3 Finely chop peanuts. Rinse chiles and discard stems. Mince chiles and mix with lime juice, sugar and sesame oil. Stir in peanuts and combine with spinach and cucumbers. Keep covered until ready to serve.

4 For the fritters: Drain corn, rinsing under cold water, then chop. Remove roots and any dark green or wilted parts from green onions, rinse rest and chop very finely. Rinse chiles and discard stems; mince rest. Peel ginger and mince or grate.

5 Rinse cilantro, shake dry, discard stems and chop leaves finely.

6 Combine corn, onions, chiles, ginger and cilantro in a bowl. Add eggs, flour and salt and stir well—briefly, but enough to combine.

7 Heat oil in a large nonstick pan. Dip a spoonful of the corn mixture out of the bowl, place in the hot oil and press a little flatter. Fry on one side over medium heat for about 3 minutes. Then turn and fry another 3 minutes (or until golden on both sides and cooked through). If you can't fit all the fritters in the pan at once, keep the finished fritters warm in an oven set to 170°F. When finished, serve with the Cucumber Spinach Salad.

Prep time: 1 hour
Delicious with: Rice, Chile Sauce (page 57) or Chinese Pancakes (page 142)
Calories per serving: 305

Vegetable Packets with Spicy Tomato Sauce

Grab one and take a bite!

Feeds 4:

For the dough:

1 3/4 cup flour plus more for working the dough

Salt

1 egg

3 tablespoons vegetable oil plus more for frying

For the sauce:

2 large ripe tomatoes

1–2 fresh red chile peppers, (e.g., Fresno, serrano, jalapeño)

4 cloves garlic

3 tablespoons grated unsweetened coconut

1 tablespoon fresh lime juice

Salt

For the filling:

5 green onions

1/2 lb. green beans

Salt

1/4 lb. shiitake or cremini mushrooms

5 leaves Chinese (napa) cabbage

1 piece ginger (3/4-inch section)

2 tablespoons vegetable oil

1/2 lb. ground beef

1 teaspoon sambal oelek

1 tablespoon soy sauce

1 egg

1 Dough: Combine flour and salt; add egg, oil and about 3 1/2 tablespoons water and mix together. Transfer the dough to a work surface—knead thoroughly until you have a soft, pliable dough that doesn't stick to your fingers. If sticky, add flour; if dry, add water. Shape into a ball, cover with a damp dishtowel and let rest 1 hour.

2 Sauce: Discard stems and cores from tomatoes and cover with boiling water in a bowl. Let stand briefly, then rinse, slip off peels, and chop. Rinse chiles, remove stems, and chop rest finely (wear gloves and don't touch your face). Peel garlic and squeeze through a press. Combine tomatoes, chiles, garlic, coconut, lime juice and salt.

3 Filling: Remove root end and any dark green or wilted parts from green onions, rinse rest and slice into rings. Rinse beans, snap off ends and cut rest into 3/4-inch pieces; boil gently in salted water for about 4 minutes. Drain and rinse with cold water.

4 Wipe off mushrooms with paper towels. Discard mushroom stems and slice caps. Rinse Chinese cabbage and cut into strips. Peel ginger and grate.

5 Heat oil and use to sauté green onions with the ginger. Add mushrooms and sauté briefly. Then add ground beef; stir-fry until crumbly. Add Chinese cabbage, then the beans, and cook a little longer until cabbage softens. Season with sambal oelek, soy sauce and salt; let cool. Briefly whisk egg and add.

6 Divide dough into eight equal pieces; roll out on a lightly floured surface into thin rectangles. Distribute filling on half of each rectangle, fold in half lengthwise and press edges together firmly; notch with a fork.

7 Heat oil, 1/2 inch deep, in a wide pan; pan-fry four parcels over medium heat for 4 minutes on each side, until golden. Keep the first batch warm on an oven-safe platter (lined with paper towels, to drain) in a 170°F oven while finishing second batch. If your pan is smaller, fry less each time and do more batches. Serve sauce alongside.

Prep time: 1 1/2 hours
Calories per serving: 630

Bok Choy with Chicken
Chinese-style cabbage

Feeds 4:

1 3/4 lbs. bok choy

1 lb. chicken breasts

1/2 teaspoon Sichuan peppercorns

1 cup chicken stock (recipe on page 58 or purchased variety)

3 tablespoons soy sauce

2 teaspoons fish sauce

Salt

3 teaspoons cornstarch

Cilantro or mint leaves for sprinkling

1 Rinse bok choy, pull off any wilted leaves and trim off core. Cut leaves lengthwise into eighths; then halve. Cut chicken into narrow strips.

2 Crush Sichuan peppercorns finely in a mortar (or extra spice/coffee grinder) and heat in a wok or pot along with chicken stock, soy sauce and fish sauce—bring to a boil. Add bok choy and chicken, return to a boil, reduce heat to medium and cover. Cook for about 4 minutes—until the bok choy is crisp-tender and the chicken is cooked throughout, with no pink remaining. Salt to taste.

3 Stir cornstarch into 3 tablespoons cold water, add to the sauce and bring to a boil. Serve with cilantro or mint leaves sprinkled on top.

Prep time: 30 minutes
Delicious with: Rice, and Spicy Cucumber Salad (see Tip on page 46) or Sichuan Vegetables (page 96)
Calories per serving: 340

Tip:
Bok choy is available in the produce section of Asian markets, some farmer's markets and some standard grocery stores. If unavailable, you can use spinach, Swiss chard or Chinese (napa) cabbage. Also, you can substitute shrimp for the chicken.

Eggplant and Oyster Sauce with Sesame Seeds
With a little bit of beef

Feeds 4:

2 smallish eggplants (about 7 oz. each)

1/3 lb. shiitake or oyster mushrooms

1/2 lb. beef tenderloin or filet

4 shallots

4 cloves garlic

1 piece ginger (3/4-inch section)

1 tablespoon fermented black beans, (Chinese grocery)

3 1/2 tablespoons sesame seeds

1/3 cup vegetable oil

3 tablespoons rice wine (sake, mirin)

3 tablespoons soy sauce

1–2 teaspoons sambal oelek

1 pinch ground cinnamon

Salt

1 teaspoon cornstarch

1 teaspoon sesame oil

1 Rinse eggplants and trim stems. Cut in quarters lengthwise, then slice those thinly crosswise. Discard mushroom stems, wipe off caps and slice. Cut beef into thin slices against the grain, and then into bite-size strips.

2 Peel shallots and slice thinly. Peel garlic and ginger and mince both. Chop black beans coarsely.

3 Heat a wok or pan. Toast sesame seeds in dry pan until a pale golden color, stirring (remove). Pour in 2 tablespoons of the oil, lightly brown the beef and remove. In the remaining oil, sauté eggplant on all sides while stirring. Add mushrooms and stir-fry for 2–3 minutes.

4 Return beef to wok or pan along with shallots, garlic, ginger, black beans and sesame seeds. Stir together rice wine, soy sauce, sambal oelek and ⅓ cup water; add. Sprinkle with cinnamon and cook uncovered for 3–4 minutes.

5 Stir cornstarch into a little cold water, stir into vegetables and return to a boil. Salt to taste. Drizzle on sesame oil and serve.

Prep time: 35 minutes
Delicious with: Rice and Cucumber Salad with Fruit (page 66) or Sichuan Vegetables (page 96)
Calories per serving: 275

Tip:

Also fantastic without meat. In this case, simply use more mushrooms or eggplant.

Stuffed Deep-Fried Eggplant
With a surprise inside, from China

Feeds 4:

1 piece ginger (¾-inch section)

4 green onions

5 oz. ground pork

1 tablespoon rice wine

Salt

2 eggplants (about ½ lb. each)

2 eggs

1½ tablespoons cornstarch

3½ cups oil for deep-frying

For the sauce:

1 teaspoon crushed red pepper flakes, (or less, to taste)

2 tablespoons rice vinegar

2 teaspoons sesame oil

¼ cup soy sauce

2 teaspoons sugar

1 Peel ginger and grate. Remove root ends and any dark green or wilted parts from green onions, rinse rest and chop finely. Mix together with grated ginger, ground pork and rice wine; season with salt.

2 Peel eggplants with a vegetable peeler and cut into ½-inch-thick rounds. Slice each round open crosswise to form a pocket that you can fill, without cutting all the way through so slices still hold together. Fill each "pocket" with a little of the meat mixture and press pocket closed.

3 Whisk together thoroughly: eggs, cornstarch and a bit of salt. Heat oil in a wide pot to 350–375°F (use oil thermometer). Meanwhile, prepare the sauce: combine pepper flakes, rice vinegar, sesame oil, soy sauce and sugar; mix well.

4 Set oven to 170°F and warm an oven-safe platter inside (lined with paper towels for draining). Dip eggplant pockets one by one into the egg mixture and then deep-fry for about 4 minutes, until golden, turning occasionally with a metal utensil. Then remove with a slotted metal utensil and transfer to the oven-warmed platter. Keep warm in oven until remaining eggplant pockets are finished.

5 Serve alongside sauce or drizzle sauce on top.

Prep time: 40 minutes
Delicious with: Cucumber Salad with Fruit (page 66, without shrimp) and rice, if desired
Calories per serving: 220

Ma Po Tofu
The Chinese
really know what
they're doing!

Feeds 4 as a full meal:

1 piece ginger ($^3/_4$-inch section)

2 green onions

4 cloves garlic

16 oz. firm tofu

3 tablespoons oil

$^1/_2$ lb. ground pork (or beef)

2–3 tablespoons black bean sauce,
(Asian grocery)

About 1 cup chicken stock (page 58)

Soy sauce for seasoning

Sesame oil for drizzling

Chili oil for drizzling

Basic Tip

Bean sauce, both mild and hot, is made from fermented black beans. The hot version also contains chiles as well as garlic and sesame oil. The mild version is available with or without garlic. To make it hotter, simply mix in 2–3 small, chopped chile peppers or some crushed red pepper flakes.

If you don't want to use a readymade sauce, buy fermented black beans and finely chop about $^1/_2$ cup. Then add the ginger, green onions and garlic listed in this Ma Po Tofu recipe. Fry all these ingredients as described in Step 2 and add stock. Finally, stir 2 teaspoons cornstarch into 1 tablespoon cold water and use to thicken the sauce. Now just season to taste with soy sauce and rice wine—ready!

1 Peel ginger and grate. Remove root end and any dark green or wilted parts from green onions, rinse rest and cut into rings. Peel garlic and mince. Cut tofu into $^1/_2$-inch cubes.

2 In a wok or pan, heat oil and briefly sauté ginger, green onions and garlic. Add ground meat and stir-fry until lightly browned and crumbly.

3 Spoon bean sauce into the wok or pan and stir. Pour in stock and heat. Then add tofu to the sauce and heat for about 5 minutes. Season to taste with soy sauce. Serve with sesame oil and hot chile oil alongside as condiments.

Prep time: 20 minutes
Delicious with: Rice
Calories per serving: 245

Tofu in Leek-Shrimp Sauce
Super-fast

Feeds 4:

12 oz. tofu

5 oz. peeled and de-veined uncooked or cooked shrimp

1 leek

1 piece ginger (1/2-inch section)

2 tablespoons oil

3 tablespoons soy sauce

3 tablespoons rice wine

1 teaspoon sugar

1 sheet nori (roasted seaweed)

1 Cut tofu into 1/2-inch cubes. Finely chop shrimp (remove tails first). Remove root end and any dark green or wilted parts from leeks, slit open lengthwise, rinse well under cold running water and chop finely; rinse again in a colander and pat dry. Peel ginger and chop very finely or squeeze through a garlic press.

2 Heat oil in a wok or pan and sauté leeks and ginger for 1–2 minutes, then stir in shrimp pieces. Combine soy sauce, rice wine, 1/3 cup water and sugar and pour into pan. Distribute tofu on top of the leeks and shrimp, cover and heat for about 2 minutes until very hot.

3 Cut nori sheet into the finest strips possible—kitchen shears work great. Stir together gently the tofu, leeks, shrimp and sauce; sprinkle with nori strips.

Prep time: 15 minutes
Delicious with: Rice or any Asian noodles
Calories per serving: 165

Also good:
Instead of leeks, use Chinese (napa) cabbage, cut into fine strips. Or, if you prefer it hot, finely chop 1–2 chile peppers and sauté with the leeks and ginger. Or, add some crushed red pepper flakes.

Spicy Hot Tofu with Curry
You have to try this one!

Feeds 4:

1 lb. tofu

3 tablespoons soy sauce

1 piece ginger (3/4-inch section)

2 cloves garlic

2 shallots

1/2 lb. snow peas

1 red bell pepper

1/3 cup oil

2 teaspoons red curry paste

1/4 cup rice wine (sake, mirin)

2 tablespoons fish sauce

2 tablespoons fresh lime juice

1 teaspoon sugar

4 sprigs basil (preferably Thai basil)

1 Cut tofu into 1/2-inch cubes and mix with soy sauce. Peel ginger, garlic and shallots. Finely chop ginger and garlic or squeeze through a garlic press. Cut shallots into fine strips or thin rings.

2 Rinse snow peas and trim ends. Rinse bell pepper, halve, remove stems and interior and cut into narrow strips.

3 Heat oil in a wok or pan and stir-fry snow peas for at least 2 minutes. Then stir in curry paste and cook for another minute.

4 Stir in bell pepper, shallots, garlic and ginger and stir-fry for 2 minutes. Add tofu, rice wine, fish sauce, lime juice and sugar. Heat for another 2 minutes.

5 In the meantime, remove basil leaves from stems. Add to pan—once the leaves have wilted the dish is finished.

Prep time: 30 minutes
Delicious preceded by and with: Rice, Crispy Spring Rolls with Shrimp Filling (page 40) and Cucumber Salad with Fruit (page 66)
Calories per serving: 310

Tofu with Mushrooms
Nice and tasty but not at all hot

Feeds 4:

1 lb. tofu

³/₄ lb. mixed mushrooms (e.g., white, shiitake, cremini and oyster mushrooms, or even just one kind)

4 cloves garlic

1 piece ginger (³/₄-inch section)

5 green onions

1 cup oil for deep-frying and sautéing

2–3 tablespoons oyster sauce

¹/₄ cup soy sauce

¹/₄ cup rice wine (sake, mirin)

¹/₂ cup chicken stock or water

2 teaspoons sesame oil

1 Cut tofu into ¹/₂-inch cubes and pat dry thoroughly with paper towels. (This will cut down on splattering while deep-frying later.)

2 Wipe off mushrooms with paper towels. Remove entire stems from shiitake and oyster mushrooms and just the ends of the stems from white mushrooms and cut rest into fine strips or thin slices. Peel garlic and ginger and chop both finely. Remove root end and any dark green or wilted parts from green onions, rinse rest and cut into fine rings. Set aside about 1 tablespoon to use as a garnish later.

3 Heat oil in a wok or pot, add tofu cubes and deep-fry for about 3 minutes until golden. Remove with a slotted metal utensil and drain on paper towels. Pour most of the oil out of the wok or pot (into another pan—once cooled, it can be sealed in a container for future use) leaving a couple tablespoons to coat the pan.

4 Briefly sauté garlic, ginger and green onions in the oil. Add mushrooms and stir-fry for 3–4 minutes. Stir together oyster sauce, soy sauce, rice wine and stock or water and pour into pot. Stir in tofu, cover and cook over low heat for 5 minutes. Sprinkle with the reserved onion rings, drizzle with sesame oil and serve!

Prep time: 40 minutes
Delicious with: Rice of any kind
Calories per serving: 310

Seafo

The fragrance of steamed ginger fish...

o d

If you like seafood, you're in for a real adventure in Asia: Fish-head curry, shark fin soup, live shrimp flambé and tuna sashimi that's as rich as a smoked side of bacon. Does all this sound a little extreme for a basic cookbook? Well, that's why we haven't included any of these recipes in the book. But there's still plenty to experience while using this book: the fragrance of freshly-steamed ginger fish, the sight of squid with papaya and mango as well as trout wrapped in banana leaves...

To keep your shopping trips from turning into major expeditions, we've applied the same policy to fish as to the other ingredients. Wherever possible we haven't recommended red snapper but simply "fish." The main thing is that it be good fish that's prepared well. After that, enjoy the adventure!

Finger Exercise No. 5
Onion Water Lilies

Mastering this exercise will train your eye to perceive treasures in unlikely places and will awaken your palate to the combination of tender and strong.

1. Take a rinsed green onion (or spring onion) with a thick bulb (gourmet grocery stores and farmer's markets) and using a knife, cut into the bottom part along the "equator," almost to its center, in a zigzag pattern so that you create a series of triangular teeth (like the top of a crown). Separate this part from the rest, shave off the root end and soak it in ice water.

2. In the same way, cut the rest of the onion into lots of "crowns" or water lilies (soak each in ice water as you work). Pat each piece dry before using—fill each with a dab of red caviar.

3. Place the "water lilies" on lily pads made from paper-thin cucumber slices. Very elegant with sushi or spicy grilled fish!

Dear Aunt Betty,

We're in Japan right now and when I think about what a big deal we make out of sushi back home, and then I taste how delicious it is here... I've already been next door to the sushi bar four times where housewives, grandfathers, school children and workers all come together—you wouldn't believe the noise! But the master behind the counter is tranquility himself. Not that he isn't working hard. He chats with me and takes our order but never loses track of what he's doing. And his sushi creations are better than anything we've ever had! Yesterday he made me my own personal sushi with raw mussels. If it had been anyone but him, I would have had serious reservations! In any case, it was interesting. It was also a great honor, apparently—someone told me that at breakfast today. For him, too, because I showed my trust in him. Rituals of respect in a fast-food joint — what a country!

Take care and see you later,

Your niece, Laura

To:
Aunt Betty
123 Homesick Lane
Des Moines, Iowa
United States

Homemade Asian Basics
Curry Paste & Powder

Is there such a thing as curry powder? No, says the connoisseur. Yes, says my grocer. What about curry paste? Yes, says the connoisseur. I don't carry it, says the grocer. Never mind, I'll just make it myself. And the powder, too.

Red curry paste: Soak 6 large dried red chiles in water for 15 minutes. Clean 2 small, fresh red chiles and chop—all the while wearing gloves and taking care not to touch your face. Toast 1 tablespoon coriander seeds, 1 teaspoon cumin seeds and 1 teaspoon shrimp paste in a dry pan until aromatic, then crush in a mortar and pestle. Peel and chop 6 cloves garlic, 1 onion and a 3/4-inch section of ginger. Grate off zest from 1 lime. Purée all these ingredients together with 1 teaspoon grated nutmeg, 1 teaspoon ground turmeric, 1 teaspoon paprika and 2 tablespoons oil. Goes great with dark meat of poultry, other meats and firm vegetables!

Green curry paste: Preparation is the same as for red except use 8 large and 2 small fresh green chiles, plus 1 cup fresh cilantro sprigs and 1 cup fresh basil sprigs. Omit ground ingredients. Works well with poultry, fish and tender vegetables.

Curry powder: Toast, in a dry pan, 1 tablespoon mustard seeds, 1 tablespoon coriander seeds, 1 tablespoon cumin seeds, 1 teaspoon black peppercorns and 6 small dried red chilies until aromatic. Then crush in a mortar and pestle and mix with 1 tablespoon turmeric. Use for Indian food.

Want less heat in any of the recipes? Just use less chiles, to your taste.

Drinking Asian Style:
Wine

With all due respect, there are good reasons why Asia and wine don't make ideal bedfellows. First, take the countryside and the climate: Tropical climate in the south, chilly temperatures in the north and gigantic mountains, rainforest, desert and ocean in between. Then consider that some Asian religions and philosophies reject alcohol. Then ponder the food itself: spicy-hot, sour, sweet and often all three together. This makes pairing wine with the food unbelievably difficult. Balance is more easily achieved with water or tea.

On the other hand, it isn't like the Asian chefs to take the easy way out. The vintners' ability to create so many different and complementary impressions from a single ingredient (grapes) is perfectly in line with the mindset of Asian cooking. "The marriage of food and wine" that Western chefs strive for sounds an awful lot like yin and yang. How could there possibly be no similarities between something as complex as wine and a cuisine as versatile as Asian?

So let's look at what the Asians have: the grassy and bitter taste of tea, the slightly sweet flavor of rice wine and the fragrance of blossom wines. Now let's look at what wine has to offer: the grassy taste of a sauvignon blanc (good with cold, herbed dishes using raw vegetables such as rice paper rolls); the slightly sweet flavor of semi-dry white wines (can be served with fruity, sour dishes) and the fragrance of a gewürztraminer (excellent with a not-too-hot curry). A good riesling can serve as an all-purpose wine that harmonizes well with the aromatic spiciness of ginger as well as the sharp sweetness of soy sauce.

The wines of Australia, California and South Africa come from regions with climates and cuisines that are similar to those of Asia, which is why these particular styles of wine often go well with Asian cuisine. Chardonnay (only lightly oak-aged) goes well with coconut-milk dishes. A weighty, aromatic shiraz can hold its own with highly flavorful dishes that are not too spicy, above all when they contain duck or beef. The rest is a matter of trial and error, or else play it safe and go with tea or beer after all (see page 39 and 127).

Steamed Ginger Fish
The whole thing!

Feeds 4:

1 large or 2 smaller whole, cleaned fish
(total of about 2 lbs.; e.g., trout)

2–3 Chinese (napa) cabbage leaves

Salt

1 large piece ginger (2-inch section)

5 green onions

2 tablespoons chicken stock

2 tablespoons soy sauce

2 tablespoons rice wine (sake, mirin)

1 tablespoon sesame oil

1 tablespoon sugar

Basil, mint or cilantro leaves for sprinkling

1 Rinse fish well under cold running water both inside and out, then pat dry thoroughly with paper towels. Rinse Chinese cabbage leaves and use to line the inside of a large bamboo steamer. Rub fish with salt inside and out and place on the leaves in the steamer.

2 Peel ginger and cut into thin slices, then into very fine strips (the finer the better). Trim root end and any wilted parts from green onions and rinse. Cut into pieces 2 inches long and then into fine strips. Combine ginger and onion strips and sprinkle over the fish.

3 Pour 1½ inches of water into the bottom of a large pot (the steamer must fit inside) and heat. Set the steamer containing the fish inside the pot. Stir together chicken stock, soy sauce, rice wine, sesame oil and sugar and spoon over the fish. Especially cover the inside of the fish.

4 Put the cover on the steamer or cover the pot if the steamer fits all the way down inside, turn heat up to high and steam fish. Steam a big fish for about 15 minutes; steam

2 smaller fish for about 10 minutes. Check periodically to make sure there's enough liquid in the pan.

5 Cut a small opening in the fish and look inside. If the fish is done, the meat will no longer be translucent and will detach easily from the bones. Detach fish from the bones in as large pieces as possible and transfer to plates (also remove skin). Pour a few spoon-fuls of the cooking liquid over the fish (strain the rest and use it as a fish stock for soup later). Sprinkle with herb leaves and serve.

Prep time: 30 minutes
Delicious with: Rice, seasoned with a mixture of chopped ginger, rice vinegar and soy sauce
Calories per serving: 175

Steamed Mussels and Shrimp
Chinese-Japanese combo

Feeds 4 or 6 as a small course:

1 piece ginger (³⁄₄-inch section)

2 cloves garlic

2 tablespoons fermented black beans

2 fresh red Fresno chiles

3 tablespoons oil

2 tablespoons spicy black bean sauce

¹⁄₂ cup rice wine

¹⁄₄ cup mirin (sweet Japanese rice wine)

3 tablespoons rice vinegar

4 shallots

8 large raw shrimp (preferably unpeeled)

2 lbs. mussels

Salt

Sesame oil for drizzling

1 Peel ginger and garlic and mince both. Chop black beans. Rinse chiles, remove stems and cut rest into fine rings (with the seeds so the sauce will be a bit spicy).

2 Heat oil in a wok or pot and sauté ginger, garlic and chiles. Add beans and bean sauce and sauté briefly. Combine rice wine, mirin and rice vinegar; add to pot and simmer sauce for about 5 to 10 minutes or until thickened.

3 Meanwhile, peel shallots, cut into thin rings and place in a bamboo steamer. Rinse shrimp and distribute over the shallots.

4 Rinse mussels thoroughly under cold running water and scrub with a brush. Any open mussels should now have closed. You must throw out any that are still open. Place the closed mussels in the steamer.

5 Pour 1¹⁄₂ inches of water into a large pot (the bamboo steamer must fit inside), bring to a boil and add salt. Set the steamer inside the pot. Cover and steam over high heat for about 5 minutes.

6 The mussels should now be open. Throw away any mussels that are still closed and transfer the rest to a platter along with the shrimp and shallots. Spoon sauce over the top, drizzle with a little sesame oil and serve.

Prep time: 50 minutes
Delicious with: Rice or Chinese Pancakes (page 142)
Calories per serving (6): 130

Tuna in Miso Marinade
Japanese food for a short break

Feeds 4:

4 tuna steaks (about 6 oz. each;

okay to substitute other types of fish)

3 tablespoons miso

¼ cup mirin (sweet Japanese rice wine)

3 tablespoons sake (Japanese rice wine)

1 tablespoon soy sauce

2 tablespoons vegetable oil (if needed)

1 Pat fish dry with paper towels; place in a bowl. Stir together miso, mirin, sake and soy sauce; pour marinade over the fish, cover, and marinate for at least 4 hours in the refrigerator. Turn the fish once halfway through.

2 Afterwards you can either grill or sauté the fish. If you want to grill it, turn on the charcoal grill or oven broiler. Then either broil the fillets or grill for about 3–4 minutes per side or until cooked through.

3 If you wish to sauté, heat oil and cook fish over medium heat for about 5 minutes on each side.

Prep time: 15 minutes
(plus 4 hours marinating time)
Delicious with and followed by: Rice and Spinach with Sesame Sauce (page 97), after which Miso Soup (page 60) goes especially well
Calories per serving: 490

Fish Fillets in Spicy Ginger Sauce
Quick and easy

Feeds 4:

5 green onions

2 shallots

4 cloves garlic

1 piece ginger (2-inch section)

1 stalk lemon grass

2 fresh red Fresno chiles

1 tablespoon oil

1 lime

Salt

1 teaspoon sugar

4 portions fish fillet (about 6 oz. each,

e.g. cod, salmon, sole, halibut)

1 Remove roots and any dark green or wilted parts from green onions and rinse rest. Peel shallots, garlic and ginger and chop all four ingredients very finely. Rinse lemon grass, cut off top and bottom ends, remove outer layer and chop rest coarsely and crush finely in a mortar or purée finely in a blender or food processor. Rinse chiles, discard stems and cut rest into very fine rings.

2 Heat oil, stir in ginger mixture and sauté for a couple minutes. Preheat oven to 350°F.

3 Rinse lime, pat dry and grate off a thin layer of zest. Squeeze juice out of half the lime. Combine ginger mixture, lime zest, lime juice, chiles and lemon grass and season this sauce with salt and add sugar.

4 Rinse fish gently and pat dry with paper towels. Place on a greased baking sheet or in a greased baking dish; coat with ginger mixture. Bake in the oven (middle rack) for about 10 minutes or until fish is opaque throughout.

Prep time: 35 minutes
Delicious with: Rice and soy sauce
Calories per serving: 405

Squid with Papaya-Mango Salad
Truly exotic

Feeds 4:

For the salad:

1 papaya

1 mango

½ cup fresh mint sprigs

½ cup fresh cilantro sprigs

2 fresh red Fresno chiles (milder),
or red serrano (hotter)

1 tablespoon fish sauce

2 tablespoons fresh lime juice

2 teaspoons sugar

For the squid:

1½ lbs. squid

1 piece ginger (¾-inch section)

2 cloves garlic

2 shallots

¼ cup oil

1 tablespoon fresh lime juice

2 teaspoons fish sauce

1 teaspoon sambal oelek (optional; use
purchased from Asian grocery, or see page 89)

Salt

1 For the salad: halve papaya and scrape out seeds. Peel both halves and cut into thin slices, then into fine strips. Peel mango, cut fruit from pit and cut into thick wedges or slices.

2 Rinse herbs, shake dry and remove any tough stems. Rinse chiles, discard stems and cut rest into fine rings. (If you like it hotter, leave in the seeds; if you want to be more cautious, remove the interior first.) Stir together fish sauce, lime juice and sugar and mix with fruit strips, chiles and herbs. Refrigerate salad until serving time.

3 Rinse squid fillets and halve lengthwise. Feel the inside of the fillets with your fingers. You will probably find a "bone" (looks like a transparent skewer) or other harder objects that you'll have to pull or cut out. Then cut squid into strips about ¼ to ½ inch wide. Peel ginger, garlic and shallots and cut into thin slices.

4 Heat oil in a wok or pan and sauté ginger, garlic and shallots. Add squid and sauté for about 4 minutes. Season to taste with lime juice, fish sauce, salt and, if desired, sambal oelek. Serve alongside the salad.

Prep time: 35 minutes
Delicious with: Rice or thin rice noodles
Calories per serving: 290

Tip:
Grilling or broiling is a clever alternative to stir-frying or sautéing. After cleaning the squid, cut into large pieces and precook in boiling, salted water for 1 minute. Then rinse under cold water. Stir together 2 tablespoons soy sauce, 2 tablespoons lime juice and 2 teaspoons honey and brush onto the squid pieces. Broil in the oven (medium rack) or grill for about 5 minutes.

Squid Curry with Greens
Nice and easy, nice and spicy

Feeds 4:

1 lb. squid

5 green onions

1/2 lb. green asparagus

12 oz. spinach

1 piece ginger (1/2-inch section)

4 cloves garlic

1/4 cup oil

2 teaspoons sambal oelek

2 teaspoons brown sugar

1/2 cup chicken or fish stock

Salt

1 Rinse squid. Feel inside the fillet tubes and remove any hard pieces of bone or cartilage you may find. Then cut squid into narrow strips or thick rings if preferred.

2 Trim off root end and any dark green or wilted parts from green onions; rinse rest. First cut into pieces about 2 inches long and then into narrower strips. Rinse asparagus, remove tough ends and cut spears on a slight angle into pieces 3/4 inch thick.

3 Rinse spinach thoroughly, removing any wilted leaves. Boil in salted water for a minute or until the leaves wilt. Rinse under cold water in a colander and drain.

4 Peel ginger and garlic and squeeze both through a garlic press. Heat oil in a wok or pan and stir-fry squid for about 4 minutes. Add ginger, garlic and green onions; stir-fry for another 2 minutes. Stir in asparagus, sambal oelek and sugar and cook for another 2 minutes.

5 Pour in stock and season with salt. Cover, reduce heat to medium and simmer for about 10 minutes. Stir in spinach and heat through. Add more sambal oelek or salt, to taste.

Prep time: 45 minutes
Delicious with: Rice and fresh cucumber slices
Calories per serving: 280

Fish Fillets with Asian Pesto
Do Italians do it better? No, just differently

Feeds 4:

For the pesto:

1 cup fresh basil sprigs

1 cup fresh mint sprigs

1 cup fresh cilantro sprigs

2 cloves garlic

1 piece ginger (3/4-inch section)

1 green onion

1 jalapeño pepper

1/3 cup unsalted peanuts

1/4 cup peanut oil

1 pinch sugar

Salt

Fresh lime juice (optional)

For the fish:

4 slices fish fillets (6 oz. each serving; e.g., halibut, cod, monkfish, sole)

1 tablespoon fresh lime juice

Salt, freshly ground pepper

8–12 cherry tomatoes

1 For the pesto, rinse herbs, shake dry and chop leaves coarsely. Peel garlic and ginger and chop both finely. Remove root end and any dark green or wilted parts from green onion; rinse rest and chop finely. Rinse jalapeño, remove stem and chop rest finely.

2 Process herbs, garlic, ginger, green onion, jalapeño and peanuts in the food processor until it forms a paste. Add peanut oil, sugar and a little salt, plus lime juice to taste.

3 For the fish, drizzle fillets with lime juice, season both sides with salt and pepper and place in a steamer (bamboo or metal). Rinse tomatoes, halve and distribute over the fish.

4 In a large pot (the steamer must fit inside), bring about 1 cup water or vegetable stock to a boil. Place the steamer in the pot, cover (either the pot or the steamer) and steam fish over high heat for about 5 minutes or until opaque throughout. Transfer to pre-warmed plates and serve, topped with the Asian pesto and accompanied by the steamed cherry tomatoes. Garnish with lime wedges.

Prep time: 30 minutes
Delicious with: Rice, rice noodles or cellophane (mung bean thread) noodles and soy sauce
Calories per serving: 450

Tip:
Like its Italian cousin, Asian pesto is extremely versatile. This spicy paste isn't just good with fish; it also works with vegetables (especially with mushrooms, green asparagus and spinach). In this case, stir-fry the vegetables in a wok, season to taste with pesto and eat with thin rice noodles or rice. Pesto with shrimp or steamed chicken also tastes great.

Fish Fillets with Grated Coconut
Practically no work at all

Feeds 4:

1 shallot

2 cloves garlic

1 piece ginger ($^3/_4$-inch section)

1 fresh red serrano chile

2 tablespoons soy sauce

2 tablespoons rice wine (sake, mirin)

2 tablespoons fresh lime juice

$^1/_2$ teaspoon ground coriander

Freshly ground pepper

8 thin fish fillets (about 1$^1/_2$ lbs. total;

e.g., sole, trout, salmon)

$^2/_3$ cup grated coconut,

(unsweetened if possible)

3 tablespoons oil

1 Peel shallots, garlic and ginger, and chop all three very finely. Rinse chiles, remove stems, and chop rest very finely (omit seeds for less heat; always wear gloves when working with chiles and don't touch your face). For the marinade, combine soy sauce, rice wine, lime juice, ground coriander and pepper. Stir in shallots, garlic, ginger and serrano.

2 Lay fish fillets side by side in a large dish, pour marinade over the top and cover. Marinate fillets in the refrigerator for at least 2 hours or up to overnight. Turn occasionally if possible.

3 Then dredge the fish fillets in grated coconut. Heat oil in a nonstick pan and pan-fry fillets over medium heat for 2 minutes. Turn carefully, fry the other side for 2 minutes or until fish is opaque throughout, and they're done!

Prep time: 25 minutes
(plus at least 2 hours marinating time)
Delicious with: Coconut Rice (page 77) and/or Spicy Tomato Sauce (see page 99)
Calories per serving: 315

Fish Curry
with Eggplant
Typical Thai

Easily feeds 4:

1 lb. firm fish fillets (e.g. swordfish, halibut, rockfish, cod, monkfish)

1 eggplant

1 small red bell pepper

1 piece ginger or galangal ($3/4$-inch section)

2 shallots

4–6 fresh kaffir lime leaves (Asian market)

2 tablespoons oil

2 tablespoons green curry paste

$1^2/_3$ cups canned coconut milk

1 tablespoon brown sugar

1 tablespoon fish sauce

Several sprigs basil (Thai basil if available)

1 With your fingers, feel the fish for bones and use tweezers to remove any you find. Cut fillets into 1-inch cubes or a little larger if preferable. Rinse eggplant, discard stem, and cut rest into small cubes. Rinse bell pepper, halve, remove contents, discard stem, and cut rest into diamonds.

2 Peel ginger or galangal and slice thinly. Peel shallots, halve and cut into strips. Rinse lime leaves and tear into pieces.

3 Heat oil in a wok or pan and sauté ginger or galangal and shallots. Stir in curry paste and sauté for 1 minute. Add coconut milk, lime leaves, brown sugar and fish sauce; simmer for about 5 minutes. The lime leaves should be releasing their aroma.

4 Stir in eggplant and bell pepper and cook for 4 more minutes. Stir in fish, reduce the heat a little and cook for another 3 minutes or until fish is opaque throughout.

5 Remove leaves from basil stems and brush off with a paper towel, if necessary. Stir leaves into curry, salt to taste and serve.

Prep time: 35 minutes
Delicious with: Rice
Calories per serving: 210

Also good:
If you like it fruity, add a few pineapple chunks or some fresh mango cubes to the curry along with the basil.

Sweet and Sour Shrimp
Fast and good

Feeds 4:

$1\frac{1}{4}$ lb. uncooked shrimp (smallish, peeled and de-veined)

2 tablespoons rice wine (sake, mirin)

2 tablespoons fresh lime juice

2 cloves garlic

1 onion

2–3 stalks celery

2 tomatoes

3 tablespoons vegetable oil

1 tablespoon brown sugar

1 tablespoon fish sauce

1 tablespoon soy sauce

1 tablespoon ketchup

1 teaspoon cornstarch

Salt

Cilantro leaves for garnish

1 Thaw, rinse and pat dry shrimp. Mix with 1 tablespoon of the rice wine and 1 tablespoon of the lime juice.

2 Peel garlic and onion. Slice garlic thinly. Halve onion and slice into strips. Rinse celery, trim ends and slice rest thinly. Rinse tomatoes, remove core and dice rest.

3 Heat oil in a wok or pan and briefly sauté celery, garlic and onion. Add shrimp and sauté for another minute.

4 Add remaining rice wine, lime juice, brown sugar, fish sauce, soy sauce, ketchup and tomatoes; simmer for 2–3 minutes. Mix cornstarch into $\frac{1}{3}$ cup water, add to pan and bring to a boil. Salt to taste, make sure shrimp are cooked through, sprinkle with cilantro and it's ready!

Prep time: 25 minutes
Delicious with: Rice
Calories per serving: 215

Fish & Vegetable Tempura
Japanese finger food

Feeds 4:

1 lb. firm-type fish fillets

(e.g., swordfish, rockfish, cod, monkfish)

$\frac{1}{3}$ lb. uncooked shrimp (peeled and deveined)

8 shiitake mushrooms

1 lb. asparagus spears (or green beans)

6 green onions

A couple Chinese (napa) cabbage leaves, (about 5 oz.)

1 quart vegetable oil for deep-frying

For the batter:

$\frac{3}{4}$ cup flour

1 egg

For the dip:

1 chunk daikon radish (about 2 inches)

1 piece ginger ($\frac{3}{4}$-inch section)

$\frac{1}{2}$ cup soy sauce

$\frac{1}{2}$ cup mirin (sweet Japanese rice wine)

$\frac{1}{4}$ cup sake (Japanese rice wine)

1 Rinse fish and pat dry with paper towels. Thaw, rinse and pat dry shrimp.

2 Wipe off mushrooms with paper towels. Discard stems. Rinse asparagus, remove the tough ends and cut rest into $\frac{3}{4}$-inch lengths. Trim off root ends and any wilted parts from green onions; rinse rest and cut into $\frac{3}{4}$-inch sections. Rinse Chinese cabbage and cut into strips.

3 For the batter: whisk together flour, $\frac{3}{4}$ cup + 2 tablespoons ice-cold water and the egg.

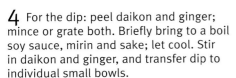

4 For the dip: peel daikon and ginger; mince or grate both. Briefly bring to a boil soy sauce, mirin and sake; let cool. Stir in daikon and ginger, and transfer dip to individual small bowls.

5 Set oven to 170°F and warm a large, oven-safe platter.

6 In a wok or pan, heat the oil for deep-frying (when you stick the handle of a wooden spoon into the oil, and a lot of tiny bubbles congregate, it's ready; or use an oil thermometer and bring to 350–375°F). Then dip some each of the fish, shrimp and then vegetables in batter; immediately place pieces in the hot oil, using a metal utensil. Don't add too many at once or the oil will cool and the batter will soak it up. When golden, remove pieces with a slotted metal utensil and lay them out on the warmed platter (line tray with paper towels). Keep warm in the oven.

7 Finish all the batches and serve dip alongside tempura.

Prep time: 1 hour
Delicious with: Japanese soba noodles
Calories per serving: 380

Saffron Fish
Indian style

In India, many dishes are made with yogurt—which is why we're using it here with the saffron fish. Don't worry if the sauce isn't perfectly smooth—the flavor of the yogurt makes up for it.

Feeds 4:

1¼ lbs. fish fillets

(e.g., cod, sole, monkfish, swordfish)

2 teaspoons fresh lemon juice

2 small onions

1 piece ginger (½-inch section)

A few threads saffron

12 cherry tomatoes

2 tablespoons oil

1 teaspoon ground turmeric

½ teaspoon ground cumin

½ teaspoon ground coriander

1 pinch ground cinnamon

¾ cup whole yogurt ("cream top"; health food stores)

Salt

1 With your fingers, feel the fish for bones and use tweezers to remove any you find. Cut fillets into ½-inch cubes and combine with lemon juice. Peel onions and ginger and chop both finely.

2 Rub saffron between your fingers and stir into ½ cup warm water. Rinse cherry tomatoes and halve each.

3 Heat oil in a wok or pan and stir in onions and ginger. Reduce heat to medium-low and sauté for about 8–10 minutes, taking care that the onions don't become too brown, which makes them taste bitter. Stir in turmeric, cumin, coriander and cinnamon and cook for another minute.

4 Pour in saffron and tomatoes. Bring to a boil momentarily and salt to taste, then carefully add fish. Turn heat to low, cover and let fish cook for 5–6 minutes (liquid should be at a simmer). Meanwhile, if your whole yogurt is a "cream top" variety, stir some of the cream down into the yogurt and mix very well. Make sure fish is cooked through (opaque throughout) and add yogurt, stirring quickly with a wooden spoon (or folding everything together with a heatproof flexible spatula). Heat the yogurt through, but do not let it boil or it will curdle. Time to serve!

Prep time: 50 minutes
Delicious with: Rice (preferably basmati) and chutney (e.g., Mango Chutney, page 75)
Calories per serving: 210

Fish Cakes with Leek and Miso
Japan-esque

Feeds 4:

1 lb. fish fillets (e.g., cod, rockfish, tuna, etc.)

1 leek

1 piece ginger (1½-inch section)

2 tablespoons sesame seeds

2 tablespoons miso (Japanese grocery)

1 egg

A little wasabi (from a tube or mixed from powder; optional)

3 tablespoons oil

1 Rinse fish and pat dry with paper towels. With your fingers, feel the fish for bones and use tweezers to remove any you find. Then chop fish very finely.

2 Trim off root end and any dark green or wilted parts from leek, slit open lengthwise, rinse very thoroughly and chop very finely. Peel ginger and chop very finely. Toast sesame seeds in a dry pan over medium heat until pale golden and aromatic; pour into a mortar and crush (or use a spice mill or grinder).

3 Combine leek, ginger, sesame seeds, miso, egg and fish. Season with salt and a little wasabi if desired. Mix together well and shape into twelve disc-like patties.

4 Heat oil in a nonstick pan and pan-fry patties over medium heat for about 4–5 minutes, then turn and repeat for about 4 minutes on the other side, until cooked through.

Prep time: 30 minutes
Delicious with: Rice, soy sauce, grated daikon radish and Japanese pickled ginger
Calories per serving: 215

Tuna with Tamarind Sauce
For lovers of Southeast Asian food

Feeds 4:

2 tablespoons tamarind paste (Asian grocery)

4 tuna steaks (about 5 oz. each)

Salt, freshly ground pepper

4 shallots

6 cloves garlic

1 fresh red Fresno chile

3 tablespoons brown sugar

1½ tablespoons fish sauce

¼ cup oil

A few fresh mint leaves for sprinkling

1 Mix tamarind in a bowl with ¾ cup hot tap water and set aside.

2 In the meantime, rinse and pat dry tuna; season on both sides with salt and pepper. Peel shallots and garlic and slice both thinly. Rinse chile, discard stem and cut rest into fine rings.

3 In a pot, heat tamarind, brown sugar and fish sauce and simmer this sauce for about 2 minutes.

4 Heat half the oil, stir in shallots, garlic and chile; sauté over medium heat until the garlic and shallots are lightly golden. Add tamarind mixture, heat through and keep sauce warm.

5 Heat remaining oil in a pan and pan-fry tuna over medium heat for 3–4 minutes on each side (add more oil as necessary). Pour sauce over the top, cover and continue to cook fish over low heat for 5 minutes. Serve with sauce spooned over the top, with fresh mint leaves as a garnish.

Prep time: 30 minutes
Delicious with: Rice
Calories per serving: 440

Variation:

Shrimp in Tamarind Sauce

Prepare tamarind sauce as described at left. Instead of garlic and shallots, rinse 1 leek well, slice into rings and sauté along with a little chopped ginger (peel ginger first). Combine with tamarind sauce. Cut ½ lb. (or about 25) cherry tomatoes in half and add. Sauté 1¼ lbs. cleaned raw shrimp (peeled and de-veined) in oil until opaque and pink. Pour sauce over the top and sprinkle with cilantro leaves.

Trout in Banana Leaves
Marvelous!

Feeds 4:

4 whole cleaned trout (about ¾ lb. each)

1 piece ginger (¾-inch section)

5 green onions

2 cloves garlic

1 tablespoon oil

1 tablespoon fresh lime juice

Salt

4-6 kaffir lime leaves (Asian grocery)

4 pieces banana leaf (each large enough for wrapping a fish—Asian grocery)

Freshly ground pepper

1 Rinse trout thoroughly both inside and out under cold running water, then pat dry with paper towels. Peel ginger and chop coarsely. Trim away root end and any dark green or wilted parts from green onions; rinse rest and chop coarsely. Peel garlic and chop coarsely.

2 Purée ginger, green onions, garlic, oil and lime juice in a blender or crush into a paste using a mortar and pestle. Season paste with salt, spread on the inside and outside of each fish and let stand for about 1 hour.

3 Preheat oven to 425°F, or start the oven broiler or light a charcoal grill. Rinse kaffir lime leaves and cut into the finest strips possible. Lay out banana leaves on the work surface (make sure they're rinsed and dried), place a few lime leaf strips in the center of each and grind a little pepper over the top. Lay the fish on top and top with more lime leaf strips and freshly ground pepper. Wrap fish well and secure with toothpicks so the packages stay intact.

4 Now either grill the trout packages for about 10 minutes on each side, broil them in the oven (middle rack) for about 30 minutes or bake on the middle oven rack at 425°F for 30 minutes.

Prep time: 40 minutes
(plus 1 hour marinating time)
Delicious with: Sambal Oelek (purchased or see page 89), Chinese Pancakes (page 142), chutney (e.g., Mango Chutney, page 75 or Coconut Chutney, page 94) and rice
Calories per serving: 190

Asian Cabbage Rolls with Fish
A great use for napa cabbage

Feeds 4:

2 fresh red Fresno chiles

3 cloves garlic

3 shallots

1 piece ginger (3/4-inch section)

1/4 cup oil

1 teaspoon ground turmeric

1 large tomato (about 1/3 lb.)

Salt

4–5 sprigs fresh cilantro

4 fish fillets (about 6 oz. each; e.g., cod, red snapper or tuna)

8 large Chinese (napa) cabbage leaves

1/2 cup canned vegetable, chicken or fish stock

1 First make the paste: Rinse chiles and remove stems. Peel garlic, shallots and ginger and chop all three finely. Heat 2 tablespoons of the oil and sauté turmeric briefly. Then sauté chopped ingredients and chiles for 2–3 minutes.

2 Rinse tomato, remove core and dice rest. Purée along with sautéed ingredient mixture in a blender or food processor; season with salt. Rinse cilantro, shake dry, chop leaves finely and stir into puréed paste.

3 Rinse and pat fish fillets dry and halve crosswise. Rinse Chinese cabbage leaves. In a wide pot, bring salted water to a boil. Boil cabbage leaves for 1-2 minutes or until leaves are pliable. Drain leaves and lay out on a work surface.

4 Spread paste on both sides of fish pieces, place on top of the cabbage leaves and wrap. Heat remaining oil in a wok or pan and pan-fry packages over medium heat for 3 minutes. Turn and cook another 3 minutes. Pour in stock and bring to a rolling boil—ready to serve.

Prep time: 35 minutes
Delicious with: Rice or rice noodles, and Cucumber Salad with Fruit (page 66)
Calories per serving: 220

Basic Tip

When used for wrapping, Chinese (napa) cabbage leaves need to be quite large. But sometimes all you can find is a small head. That's okay, it just means you'll have to use a little more ingenuity. Simply remove more leaves from the head and precook them. Then cut the fish into smaller pieces, spread the pieces with paste and wrap them in the leaves. You might even like them better than the larger cabbage rolls.

Meat &

Not just with sauce but in the best of company....

Poultry

Chicken, pork, beef, lamb and a few other animals we'd rather not mention here are all welcome on Asian dinner tables, not as just a dull solo act with a sauce, but as a member of an orchestra with an accompaniment of ingredients such as vegetables, starches, pastry and even fish.

This meat or poultry is typically served bite-size, accompanied by rice. These substantial meat, rice and vegetable dishes will have you feeling nicely full, just exactly right, and just satisfied enough so that you'll soon be ready to think about the next meal. And, that's the way it should be.

Finger Exercise No. 6
Cucumber Fans

As you master this exercise, your hands will acquire a steadiness of hand and a sense of when it's time to stop.

1. Cut a cucumber in half lengthwise and cut off the ends of the two halves at an angle. With a sharp knife, slice the cucumber as thinly as possible six times, cutting in just far enough so that the slices are still attached to one another.

2. With the seventh cut, sever the section (which is about to become a fan) from the cucumber. Now fold in every other slice and wedge it between the other slices.

3. Cut the whole cucumber likewise, into fans. The fans can also consist of more or less than six slices. They're beautiful with roasted meats, fish, vegetable dishes or with any appetizers.

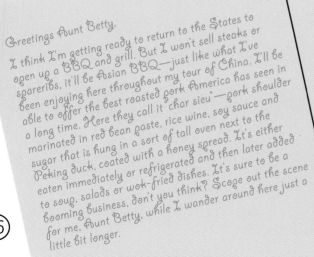

Greetings Aunt Betty,

I think I'm getting ready to return to the States to open up a BBQ and grill. But I won't sell steaks or spareribs, it'll be Asian BBQ—just like what I've been enjoying here throughout my tour of China. I'll be able to offer the best roasted pork America has seen in a long time. Here they call it "char siew"—pork shoulder marinated in red bean paste, rice wine, soy sauce and sugar that is hung in a sort of tall oven next to the Peking duck, coated with a honey spread. It's either eaten immediately or refrigerated and then later added to soup, salads or wok-fried dishes. It's sure to be a booming business, don't you think? Scope out the scene for me, Aunt Betty, while I wander around here just a little bit longer.

See you,

Your jet-set nephew, Walter

To:
Aunt Betty
123 Homesick Lane
Des Moines, Iowa
United States

12.06.2002
POST
Basic Services
5

Homemade Asian Basics
Master Stock

Every good Chinese chef keeps this potion in his kitchen—then, every day during his lifetime he can cook up to-die-for chicken in the stock... which, of course, creates more stock. Every day he stretches the stock further and further, using stock but cooking more chicken and adding more liquid—until he finally retires and leaves his master stock to his children or successor. It's true!

For 1 chicken (3¼ lbs.), bring to a boil 6 cups water, 1 cup light soy sauce, 1 cup rice wine (sake, mirin) and ¼ cup sugar. Peel 1 piece ginger (2-inch section) and 3 cloves garlic and cut both into slices. Add to water along with 4 star anise and 2 cinnamon sticks, bring to a boil and then reduce heat; simmer for 30 minutes.

Now place the chicken in the water, breast-side down, and simmer gently for 20 minutes. Then turn and simmer another 5 minutes or until chicken is cooked through, opaque and juices run clear. Remove pot from heat, partially cover and let chicken cool in the liquid.

The slightly aromatic meat of the chicken can be used in soups, salads and appetizers. The stock can be strained and stored (refrigerated for a week or frozen for months)—just add more water and a little more of the ingredients above and use to cook the next chicken!

Drinking Asian Style:
Beer

Now that we're approaching the end, we can finally say it: Asia's national drink isn't green tea, rice wine or water from a clear village spring. It's beer. Most of its beers are light—in the beginning they still did a lot with rice but now the main ingredients are mostly barley, malt and hops.

And, in fact, a cold, sparkling, light Asian beer with its slightly sweet flavor (often due to a little rice) is a great companion to the continent's light but spicy dishes. If you combine a dish containing the flavors typical of a particular country with that country's own beer, you really can't go wrong.

China's most famous beer is the somewhat malty Tsingtao, which was originally established by German brewers in western China. Japan's Kirin brewery sent its brew master to be trained in Bavaria. Today the two other most important breweries on the island are Asahi and Sapporo. India produces the refreshing Kingfisher and Thailand the more bitter Singha. Malaysia, or rather Singapore, produces one of the most popular beers on the international market—Tiger Beer. Vietnam's 33 and Indonesia's Bintang are harder to find.

Now all you have to decide is which is more authentic: Drinking Tsingtao with "chicken with seven delicacies" and Kirin with yakitori, or just drinking your own favorite beer with any Asian food. Up to you!

Satay Skewers
Finger food for indoors or out

Feeds 4:

1½ lbs. meat (pork, chicken breast or leg of lamb)

1 piece ginger (¾-inch section)

¼ cup soy sauce

¼ cup kecap manis (sweet, seasoned soy sauce found in Asian markets)

2 tablespoons oil (if sautéing)

For the peanut sauce:

¾ cup roasted salted peanuts

2 tablespoons oil

2 tablespoons red curry paste

1 cup canned coconut milk

2 tablespoons brown sugar

Salt

2 tablespoons fresh lime juice

1 Slice meat very thinly and thread it back and forth onto long wooden or metal skewers like an accordion. Peel ginger, grate finely, and mix with soy sauce and kecap manis; distribute over skewers. Cover and marinate for about 2 hours or longer, refrigerated.

2 For the sauce, chop peanuts or grind in a blender or food processor. Heat oil in a pan and add red curry paste; sauté briefly. Add coconut milk, ½ cup water, peanuts and sugar; simmer over medium heat for 10–15 minutes. Season sauce to taste with salt and lime juice; let cool to lukewarm.

3 Cook the skewers either on a charcoal grill, under an oven broiler or in a pan with oil over high heat. In any case, cook only until the meat is lightly browned (make sure pork and chicken are cooked throughout). Serve peanut sauce alongside.

Prep time: 50 minutes
(plus 2 hours marinating)
Delicious with: Rice and Spicy Cucumber Salad (page 46)
Calories per serving: 540

Variation:

Yakitori Skewers

In a pot, combine ⅓ cup sake (Japanese rice wine), ⅓ cup mirin (sweet Japanese rice wine), ⅓ cup soy sauce and 2 tablespoons sugar and reduce until thick and syrupy and starting to foam. Clean 2 thin leeks by slitting open lengthwise and rinsing very thoroughly; cut on a slight angle into ½-inch pieces. Cut 1⅓ lbs. chicken breast into pieces ½ inch thick and 1 inch long. Alternately thread chicken and leek onto long wooden or metal skewers; brush on sauce. You can then grill them or cook under the oven broiler for about 10 minutes. Or if all else fails, sauté in a pan with a little vegetable oil. In any case, brush them frequently with more sauce while they cook.

Meatballs with Chile Sauce
Made to be dipped

Feeds 4:

3 green onions

½ cup fresh mint sprigs

1 piece ginger (½-inch section)

1⅓ lbs. ground pork

1 tablespoon mirin (sweet Japanese rice wine)

1 tablespoon sake (Japanese rice wine)

1 tablespoon soy sauce

1 egg white

3 cups oil for deep-frying

For the sauce:

2 fresh red Fresno chiles or red jalapeños

2 green onions

2 tablespoons fish sauce

3 tablespoons light rice vinegar

and/or fresh lime juice

1 For the meatballs: Trim off root end and any dark green or wilted parts from green onions, rinse rest, halve lengthwise and slice finely crosswise. Rinse mint, shake dry and chop leaves finely. Peel ginger and grate or squeeze through a garlic press.

2 Combine ground meat with the green onions, mint and ginger plus the mirin, sake, soy sauce and egg white; mix thoroughly. Roll mixture between your hands and shape into walnut-sized balls.

3 For the sauce: Rinse chiles, discard stems and cut rest into very fine rings. Then briefly chop these rings. Again, trim off root end and any dark green or wilted parts from green onions, rinse rest and chop very finely. Combine fish sauce with vinegar and/or lime juice and 2 tablespoons water, stir in chopped chiles and green onions; transfer sauce to individual bowls.

4 Heat the oil for deep-frying in a wok or pot. Test it by sticking the handle of a wooden spoon in the oil; when a lot of tiny bubbles dance around it, the oil is hot enough (Or use an oil thermometer—should register 350–375°F). Immediately reduce the heat to medium. (If the oil is too hot, the meatballs will burn on the outside and be raw on the inside.) Using a slotted metal utensil, place the meatballs in the oil in two or three batches and fry for about 5 minutes per batch. Remove with metal utensil, drain on a paper-towel lined plate (check to make sure they're cooked through) and serve with the sauce.

Prep time: 40 minutes
Delicious with: Cellophane (mung bean thread) noodles, softened and eaten chilled—in this case, double the sauce recipe or simply place soy sauce, Chile Sauce (page 57) and Sambal Oelek (page 89) on the table and let guests help themselves
Calories per serving: 260

Sukiyaki
Japanese for "cooked at the table"

The meat is fried in oil at the table: use a portable gas or electric burner and a heavy pot (or a fondue pot). Otherwise, prepare everything in a wok in the kitchen and serve the finished product. Make sure to make some rice to go with it.

Feeds 4:

1½ lbs. beef tenderloin, filet, or ribeye

3½ oz. cellophane (mung bean thread) noodles

8 oz. tofu

1 small head Chinese (napa) cabbage

2 handfuls spinach

2 small leeks (or 6 green onions)

⅓ lb. fresh shiitake mushrooms

4 very fresh eggs (optional)

¼ cup vegetable oil

For the seasoning sauce:

½ cup dashi stock (page 59 or instant or chicken stock)

½ cup soy sauce

½ cup rice wine (sake, mirin)

2 tablespoons sugar

1 Prepare ingredients ahead of time for cooking at the table: freeze beef for one hour, then slice thinly. Cover cellophane noodles with water until soft; drain. Cut tofu into ¾-inch cubes. Rinse napa cabbage and cut into 1-inch strips. Rinse spinach well, drain and discard any tough stems. Trim leeks, halve lengthwise, rinse very well and slice crosswise thinly. Wipe off mushrooms with paper towels, discard stems and slice caps. Arrange ingredients on platters.

2 Sauce: bring to a boil dashi, soy sauce, rice wine and sugar together—pour into a pitcher or glass measuring cup. Whisk the eggs and portion out to four individual bowls at each place setting. (Do not serve to young children, elderly or anyone with a compromised immune system, as eggs will be consumed partially raw)

3 Heat pot on table top burner and add oil. First sauté a little meat that has been drizzled with a small amount of sauce. Then add tofu and vegetables, then a few cellophane noodles and, finally, a little sauce. After a few minutes, the first ingredients are ready for the taking. Dip cooked items in egg briefly (if desired), then eat with rice. Keep adding ingredients and sauce to the pot.

Prep time: 35 minutes
Delicious with: Rice, sake and cold Japanese beer
Calories per serving: 695

Deep-Fried Pork Ribs
Extremely addictive

Be sure to start these well ahead of time to allow for 12 hours of marinating.

Feeds 4:

1 large piece ginger (2-inch section)

4 cloves garlic

3 tablespoons honey

2 teaspoons sesame oil

¼ cup soy sauce

½ cup black bean sauce

3½ lbs. spareribs (with a lot of meat; have butcher cut them into pieces about 4 inches long)

4 cups oil for deep-frying

For the Chinese cabbage:

1 small head Chinese (napa) cabbage

1 large onion

2 tablespoons oil

½ cup chicken stock (page 32), or vegetable stock (purchased okay)

2 tablespoons soy sauce

2 tablespoons rice vinegar

1 tablespoon Sambal Oelek (page 89 or purchased) or Chinese chile-garlic sauce or Chile Sauce (page 57)

1 Peel ginger and garlic; squeeze both through a garlic press. Mix with honey, sesame oil, soy sauce and black bean sauce to form the marinade. Rinse spareribs, pat dry, and cut apart individual ribs. Brush with marinade, cover and refrigerate for 12 hours.

2 Shortly before you plan on cooking ribs: Rinse napa cabbage well and cut into ³/₄-inch strips. Peel onion, halve and cut into strips. Heat oil in a pan and sauté onion for 2 minutes. Add napa cabbage and sauté briefly; remove from heat. Resume cooking while you're in the middle of cooking the ribs: add stock, soy sauce, rice vinegar and Sambal Oelek or other chile sauce to cabbage mixture. Cover and simmer over very low heat until cabbage is crisp-tender (make sure it doesn't get mushy).

3 Heat oil for deep-frying in a wok or deep pot (to 350–375°F, using an oil thermometer). Or, test by sticking the handle of a wooden spoon in the oil; when many tiny bubbles congregate around it, the oil is ready. Reduce heat to medium. Place the ribs in the oil in batches and deep-fry for 6 minutes each batch. Remove with a slotted metal utensil and fry the next batch likewise.

4 Transfer the ribs to a platter lined with paper towels—place in a 170°F oven to keep warm.

5 When all the ribs are ready, salt napa cabbage mixture to taste and serve alongside ribs.

Prep time: 30 minutes
(plus at least 12 hours marinating time)
Delicious with: Rice and cold Asian beer
Calories per serving: 960

Chicken with Cashews
Genuinely spicy!

Feeds 4 as a full meal:

1¹/₃ lbs. chicken breasts

1 egg white

1 tablespoon cornstarch

Salt

1–2 red bell peppers

5 green onions

2 cloves garlic

4–6 fresh red Fresno chile peppers or red jalapeños

3 tablespoons soy sauce

2 tablespoons rice wine (sake, mirin)

2 tablespoons rice vinegar

2 teaspoons sugar

1 teaspoon sesame oil

¹/₃ cup vegetable oil

²/₃ cup cashews

1 Cut chicken breasts into ¹/₂-inch cubes. Mix with egg white, cornstarch and a little salt.

2 Rinse bell peppers, halve, discard stems, remove seeds and ribs and cut rest into strips. Remove root ends and any dark green or wilted parts from green onions, rinse rest and slice into thin rings. Peel garlic. Rinse chiles and discard stems. Finely mince garlic and chiles together (wear gloves and don't touch your face). For the sauce: combine soy sauce, rice wine, rice vinegar, sugar and sesame oil in a small bowl.

3 Heat wok or pan, add oil and fry cashews for about 1 minute until golden. Remove with a slotted metal utensil, drain well on paper towels and set aside.

4 Add bell peppers, green onions and the garlic-chile mixture to the oil, and fry over high heat for 30 seconds to 1 minute. Add chicken and stir-fry for about 2 minutes or until cooked through. Pour in sauce, add cashews, heat through and serve.

Prep time: 20 minutes
Delicious with: Rice
Calories per serving: 470

Lamb with Oyster Sauce
Elegantly Chinese

Feeds 4 as a full meal:

1 lb. tender lamb, (e.g., from the leg, without bone)

1/2 tablespoon cornstarch

1 tablespoon rice wine (sake, mirin)

Salt

1 leek

10 oz. fresh mushrooms (e.g., shiitake, oyster, cremini or white mushrooms)

1 piece ginger (1/2-inch section)

2 cloves garlic

2 tablespoons soy sauce

3 tablespoons oyster sauce

1 teaspoon sugar

1 teaspoon sesame oil

1/4 cup canola or vegetable oil

1 First slice meat thinly, removing any sinews or significant fat. Then cut slices into thin strips. Mix together cornstarch, rice wine, 1 tablespoon water and a little salt. Stir in meat and set aside.

2 Trim off root end and any dark green or wilted parts from leek, slit open lengthwise, rinse thoroughly (between every layer) and cut into rings 1/2 inch thick. Remove entire stems from shiitake and oyster mushrooms or just the ends of the stems from cremini or white mushrooms. Wipe off mushrooms with paper towels and slice or cut into strips. Peel ginger and garlic and mince both.

3 Stir together soy sauce, oyster sauce, sugar and sesame oil into a sauce until the sugar dissolves. Heat a wok or pan until hot and pour in oil and heat.

4 Add lamb to wok and immediately start stirring. After about 1–2 minutes, the strips should have mostly cooked through. Remove meat from the wok. Briefly stir-fry ginger and garlic, then add sliced leek and mushrooms; stir-fry for about another 2 minutes.

5 Return lamb strips to the pan and add sauce. Stir well, taste and add salt if necessary. Ready to serve!

Prep time: 20 minutes
Delicious with: Rice
Calories per serving: 575

Lamb with Eggplant and Red Lentils
Elegantly Indian

Feeds 4 as a full meal:

1 lb. lamb (e.g., leg, lean shoulder or breast without bone)

1 eggplant

2 onions

1 piece ginger (3/4-inch section)

2 fresh red Fresno chiles

4 tomatoes

1/4 cup clarified butter or ghee (specialty store, or make your own by melting butter and skimming and discarding any white solids that rise to the surface)

1 teaspoon ground turmeric

1 teaspoon Hungarian paprika

1 teaspoon ground cumin

3/4 cup red lentils

1 tablespoon fresh lemon juice

1 teaspoon sugar

Salt

Garam masala for sprinkling

1 Cut lamb into 1-inch cubes, removing thick pieces of fat and sinews. Rinse eggplant, discard stem and cut rest into 1-inch cubes. Peel onions and chop. Peel ginger and grate. Rinse chiles, discard stems and slice rest thinly. Rinse and core tomatoes, and cut into eighths.

2 Heat clarified butter in a dutch oven (or other sturdy pot with a lid), and sauté turmeric, paprika and cumin for about 1 minute. Add eggplant and sauté briefly. Stir in onions, ginger and chiles. Add lamb and lentils; sauté briefly.

3 Stir in tomatoes, 2 cups water (or stock), lemon juice and sugar. Cover and simmer over medium heat for 1 hour or until lamb is tender, stirring occasionally. Salt to taste. Also, season with garam masala to taste.

Prep time: 1 hour 30 minutes
(1 hour of which is stewing time)
Delicious with: Plain rice or Saffron Almond Rice (page 77)
Calories per serving (4): 670

Braised Anise Pork
Chinese comfort food

Feeds 4:

10 dried shiitake mushrooms

1 3/4 lbs. lean pork (e.g., tenderloin, loin roast or chop)

1 piece ginger (1 1/2-inch section)

4 cloves garlic

4 shallots

1/4 cup oil

1/4 cup brown sugar

1/4 cup soy sauce

1/2 cup rice wine

4 star anise

3 sticks cinnamon

4 green onions

Salt

Sesame oil for drizzling

1 Place mushrooms in a bowl, cover with hot water and let soak for about 20 minutes until softened. Meanwhile: cut lean pork into 3/4-inch pieces. Peel ginger, garlic and shallots and slice thinly. When the mushrooms are soft, drain and trim off stems.

2 Heat oil to a high temperature in a wok or pan and sauté pork very well in two batches, then remove. Pour sugar into oil and stir to melt it. Add soy sauce and rice wine and stir well with a wooden spoon. Return pork to the pan and add ginger, garlic and shallots. Add mushrooms, star anise and cinnamon along with enough water to cover the ingredients.

3 Cover and stew over low heat for about 2 hours until the meat is very tender and the liquid has been reduced by half.

4 Then trim away root ends and any dark green or wilted parts from green onions, rinse rest and cut into fine rings. Salt pork to taste. If necessary, reduce the sauce even more over high heat. Before serving, sprinkle meat with green onion pieces and drizzle with sesame oil.

Prep time. 2 hours 40 minutes
(2 hours of which is stewing time)
Delicious with: Rice and fresh cucumber slices
Calories per serving: 755

Beef with Mandarin Oranges
Worth the effort!

In China, this exquisite dish is prepared with dried and soaked mandarin orange peels. In this recipe, we call for canned mandarin oranges—you can also use fresh mandarin oranges along with a bit of fresh mandarin orange peel zest.

Feeds 4:

1⅓ lbs. beef tenderloin, filet, or ribeye

2 leeks

1 piece ginger (½-inch section)

¾ cup canned mandarin orange sections

¼ cup oil

½ to 1 teaspoon crushed red pepper flakes, (to your taste)

2 teaspoons Sichuan peppercorns (optional—Chinese grocery)

2 tablespoons rice wine

¼ cup soy sauce

½ cup chicken stock

1 tablespoon sugar

Salt

⅓ cup mandarin orange juice

1 Slice the meat paper thin with a sharp knife—to make this job easier, freeze the beef for 1 hour before slicing.

2 Trim away root end and any dark green or wilted parts from leek, slit open lengthwise, rinse very well and slice thinly crosswise.

Peel ginger and mince. Drain mandarin oranges in a strainer, being careful to save the juice.

3 Heat the oil to very hot in a wok or pan and fry the meat in two or three batches until crispy. (If you throw it all in the wok at once, it won't brown well due to too much moisture.) Drain each batch on a paper-towel lined plate.

4 In remaining oil, sauté leek, ginger, crushed red pepper flakes and Sichuan peppercorns (if using). Add rice wine, soy sauce and stock; bring to a rolling boil. Return meat to the pan and season to taste with sugar and a little salt. At the very end, stir in mandarin oranges and ⅓ cup mandarin orange juice and heat. Add more mandarin juice, if necessary, to create more sauce. Ready!

Prep time: 30 minutes to 1 hour
Delicious with: Rice
Calories per serving: 360

Basic Tip

Sichuan peppercorns have little in common with the peppercorns that fill our peppermills. They look different, taste different and are unrelated. Sichuan peppercorns are actually the berries and pods from a Chinese prickly ash tree. For cooking you can either throw the whole peppercorns into the dish (then simply spit them out or chew them up!) or crush them finely in a mortar and season the dish with the powder. The Sichuan peppercorns have a numbing effect on the tongue, which some find distasteful—others are crazy about this ingredient. You can also sauté the kernels in oil, remove them and then sizzle all your other ingredients in this infused oil. But in this last case, the taste is pretty mild—however, you'll avoid the numbing affect.

Spicy Beef with Lemon Grass
Very easy and very good

Feeds 4:

1½ lbs. beef tenderloin, filet, ribeye

1 tablespoon soy sauce

1 teaspoon fish sauce

2 stalks lemon grass

4 cloves garlic

1 piece ginger (¾-inch section)

3 fresh red Fresno chile peppers

5 green onions

⅔ lb. tomatoes

¼ cup vegetable oil

½ cup Asian chicken stock (page 58), or purchased

1 teaspoon sugar

1 tablespoon kecap manis (sweet soy sauce, Asian grocery)

Salt

Cilantro leaves for garnish

1 Using a sharp knife, slice beef as thinly as possible against the grain. Then cut slices into bite-size pieces. Combine meat with soy and fish sauces.

2 Rinse lemon grass, trim ends, remove outer layer and finely chop the rest. Peel garlic and chop. Peel ginger and chop. Process lemon grass, garlic, and ginger in a small food processor, blender (add a bit of water if necessary) or mince together finely.

3 Rinse chiles, discard stems and slice rest finely into rings. Remove root ends and any dark green or wilted parts from green onions, rinse rest and cut into 1½-inch lengths; then halve these pieces lengthwise. Core and rinse tomatoes, then dice.

4 Heat oil in a wok or large pan and stir-fry meat for 2 minutes. Remove (set aside) and add green onions and chiles to the pan; sauté for 1 minute. Stir in lemon grass mixture and tomatoes. Add stock, sugar and kecap manis. Return meat to pan, heat through thoroughly and salt to taste. Garnish with cilantro and serve.

Prep time: 25 minutes
Delicious with: Rice or rice noodles, and chopped, roasted salted peanuts
Calories per serving: 320

Pork in Spicy Caramel Sauce
Cook the meat the day before

Feeds 4:

1½ lbs. pork for stewing (e.g., shoulder; ask butcher)

1⅔ cups chicken stock (page 32 or purchased)

4 chile peppers (mixture of mildly hot Fresnos and medium-hot jalapeños)

1 piece ginger (¾-inch section)

3 tablespoons brown sugar

¼ cup oil

1 tablespoons fish sauce

2 tablespoons fresh lime juice

1 Add to pot: pork, chicken stock, and 2 cups water; bring to a boil. Cover and simmer over low heat for 1½ to 2 hours. (liquid should look like it's just about to boil, but not be rapidly boiling). Meat should be tender; if not, let it cook a little longer. Let cool in the liquid.

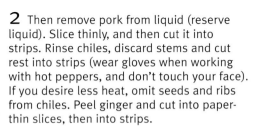

2 Then remove pork from liquid (reserve liquid). Slice thinly, and then cut it into strips. Rinse chiles, discard stems and cut rest into strips (wear gloves when working with hot peppers, and don't touch your face). If you desire less heat, omit seeds and ribs from chiles. Peel ginger and cut into paper-thin slices, then into strips.

3 In a pot, heat brown sugar and ½ cup of the cooking liquid until the sugar dissolves. Add chiles and ginger; simmer briefly.

4 Heat oil in a wok or pan and fry meat strips in batches (about 4) until nice and brown, then remove. When all the meat strips have been fried, return them to the wok and add the brown sugar sauce. Lastly, season with the fish sauce, lime juice and salt (to taste); bring to a boil. Ready!

Prep time: 25 minutes
(plus 1½–2 hours stewing time)
Delicious with: Rice and Spicy Bean
Sprouts with Coconut (page 91)
Calories per serving: 350

Beef with Sesame Sauce
Really easy

Feeds 4:

1⅓ lbs. beef tenderloin, filet, or ribeye

1 small leek

1 piece ginger (¾-inch section)

2 tablespoons rice wine (sake, mirin)

3 tablespoons soy sauce

1 teaspoon sugar

¼ cup sesame seeds

2 tablespoons oil

¼ cup stock (chicken or beef)

1 teaspoon sesame oil

1 Freeze meat for 30 minutes, then slice as thinly as possible with a very sharp knife.

2 Remove root end and any wilted or dark green parts from leek, slit open lengthwise, rinse thoroughly and chop finely. Peel ginger and grate finely.

3 Mix beef with leek, ginger, rice wine, 1 tablespoon of the soy sauce and sugar; marinate briefly.

4 Meanwhile, pour sesame seeds into a dry wok or pan and toast until golden, stirring. Crush lightly in a mortar or spice mill (or use blender or food processor).

5 Heat oil in a wok or pan and stir-fry beef in three batches, each for about 2 minutes. When batches are finished, return all beef to the pan. Add sesame seeds and stock. Season to taste with remaining soy sauce, and drizzle with sesame oil.

Prep time: 20 minutes
(plus 30 minutes freezing time)
Delicious with: Rice and fresh
cucumber slices
Calories per serving: 300

Sweet and Sour Pork
Chinese restaurant classic

Feeds 4:

1 1/2 lbs. lean pork

2 tablespoons cornstarch

2 tablespoons rice wine

1 egg

Salt

1 red bell pepper

1/2 cucumber (or 4-inch section)

1 leek

1 piece ginger (3/4-inch section)

2 cloves garlic

3 tablespoons sugar

3 tablespoons rice vinegar

2 tablespoons rice wine (sake, mirin)

2 tablespoons soy sauce

2 tablespoons tomato sauce or ketchup

2 1/2 cups oil for deep-frying and sautéing

1 Cut pork into 1/2-inch slices, then into 1/2-inch strips. Whisk together: cornstarch, rice wine, egg and 1 pinch salt. Combine mixture together with meat.

2 Rinse bell pepper, halve lengthwise, discard stem and remove seeds and ribs. Cut into diamonds, squares or rectangles. Rinse cucumber piece, halve lengthwise, scrape out seeds and slice rest crosswise thinly. Remove root end and any wilted or dark green parts from leek, slit rest open lengthwise, rinse well and slice crosswise thinly. Peel ginger and garlic; mince both.

3 Mix the following together to form the sauce: sugar, rice vinegar, rice wine, soy sauce and tomato sauce or ketchup.

4 Set oven to 200°F and warm an oven-safe platter in it (lined with paper towels). Heat oil in a hot wok or deep pot (to 350–375°F using an oil thermometer), and deep-fry pork strips in batches for about 3 minutes each. Remove with a slotted metal utensil, lay out on the paper towel-line platter and keep warm in the oven while finishing remaining batches.

5 When the pork batches are finished, pour all the oil out of the wok or pot except for a thin coating (pour it into another pot, let it cool, then strain it and pour into a container for future use). Sauté bell pepper in pan for 1 minute. Add leek, cucumber, ginger and and garlic; sauté another minute. Pour in sauce and heat through. Return the pork to the pan, heat through and serve immediately.

Prep time: 35 minutes
Delicious with: Rice
Calories per serving: 485

Variation:

This time with pineapple

Pour 1 can pineapple chunks (8 oz. drained and cut if necessary) into a colander and drain, setting aside 1/3 cup pineapple juice. Stir together juice, 1 tablespoon cornstarch, 2 tablespoons kecap manis (sweet soy sauce), 2 tablespoons rice vinegar and freshly ground black pepper (coarse) to create sauce. Cut 1 1/3 lbs. pork or chicken breasts into very thin strips, press slightly flat and mix with sauce. Marinate for 1 hour. Rinse 5 green onions, remove any dark green or wilted parts and cut into 2-inch lengths, then into thin strips. Rinse 1 tomato, remove core and cut in half, then into strips. Heat 2 tablespoons oil in a wok or pan and sauté onion strips until lightly browned. Add meat including marinade, cover and simmer over medium heat for 2 minutes. Stir in pineapple chunks and tomato, cover again and simmer for 2 more minutes.

Tandoori Chicken
Must be nice and red

Easily feeds 4:

1 3/4 lb. chicken breasts

Juice from 2 lemons

Drops red food coloring

Salt

1 piece ginger (3/4-inch section)

3 cloves garlic

1 teaspoon each of ground cumin, ground coriander, Hungarian paprika and freshly grated nutmeg

1 teaspoon ground turmeric

1/2 teaspoon chili powder

1/2 teaspoon freshly ground pepper

1 3/4 cups yogurt

1 Make sure to start the night before. Make slits in chicken breasts about 1/8 inch deep, spaced 3/4 inch apart. Place in a bowl. Combine lemon juice and many drops of red food coloring; pour over chicken. It should look very red. Season with salt and let stand for about 30 minutes.

2 Peel ginger and garlic. Squeeze both through a garlic press; stir into yogurt along with all the other spices. Pour yogurt sauce over chicken, mix well, cover and marinate overnight, refrigerated.

3 On the next day, preheat oven to 350°F. Cover a baking sheet with aluminum foil. Remove chicken pieces from marinade (reserve marinade), arrange side by side on the baking sheet and bake in the oven (middle rack) for about 35 minutes (reserve marinade). Halfway through and then once more before finished, turn chicken and brush with more marinade. Make sure chicken is cooked through before serving.

Prep time: 15 minutes (plus overnight marinating time and 35 minutes in the oven)
Delicious with: Rice
Calories per serving: 290

Tip:
In India (where this recipe comes from) they never serve a chicken with rice alone; there also must be a few sauces. Yogurt with a lot of chopped fresh mint and maybe a little chili powder tastes especially good, as does chutney. You can buy prepared chutney from an Asian market or well-stocked standard supermarket—or, make it yourself using the recipes on pages 75 and 94 (which, of course, is much more impressive).

Lemon Chicken
Ready in a jiffy!

Feeds 4:

1 1/2 lbs. chicken breasts

1 piece ginger (1/2-inch section)

2 shallots

2 lemons

1 cup oil for deep-frying and frying

1/4 cup honey

3 tablespoons rice wine

3 tablespoons soy sauce

1/4 cup chicken stock

Salt

Cilantro leaves for sprinkling

1 Cut chicken breasts into 1-inch cubes, then pat dry with paper towels so they don't splatter later when they're deep fried. Peel ginger, cut into thin slices and then cut into fine strips. Peel shallots and slice thinly.

2 Rinse one of the lemons, pat dry and peel off a thin layer of zest (without the white part). Cut peel into very fine strips (or use a zester from the beginning). Squeeze juice out of both lemons.

3 Heat oil to very hot in a wok or pan (when you insert a wooden spoon handle into the oil, there should be lots of tiny bubbles), add half the chicken cubes and deep-fry while stirring until they're golden and crispy looking. Then remove with a slotted metal utensil and drain on a paper-towel lined plate. Deep-fry the rest of the chicken in the same way, remove from the oil and drain.

4 Pour all the oil out of the wok or pan except for about 3 tablespoons (pour into another container until it cools—then discard). Sauté ginger, lemon peel and sliced shallots briefly while stirring. Add honey and let it melt. Combine lemon juice, rice wine, soy sauce and stock—and then add.

5 Let the honey-lemon sauce bubble until it becomes slightly syrupy. Stir in chicken cubes and heat well. Salt to taste, sprinkle with cilantro leaves and serve.

Prep time: 20 minutes
Delicious with: Rice, and Spinach with Sesame Sauce (page 97)
Calories per serving: 400

Walnut Chicken
Super easy, super tasty

Feeds 4:

$1\frac{1}{3}$ lbs. chicken breasts

2 teaspoons cornstarch

$\frac{1}{4}$ cup rice wine (sake, mirin)

5 green onions

1 piece ginger ($\frac{3}{4}$-inch section)

$\frac{2}{3}$ cup walnuts

$\frac{1}{4}$ cup vegetable oil

3–4 tablespoons soy sauce

1 Cut chicken breasts into $\frac{3}{4}$-inch cubes. Stir cornstarch into 2 tablespoons of the rice wine and mix well with the chicken cubes.

2 Remove root ends and any dark green or wilted parts from green onions and rinse rest; cut into $\frac{3}{4}$-inch lengths. Peel ginger, slice thinly and then slice into matchsticks. Break walnuts into small pieces or chop coarsely.

3 Heat oil in a wok or pan, add walnuts and stir-fry for 1–2 minutes or until golden. Remove from oil and set aside.

4 Add chicken to the pan and stir-fry for 1 minute. Add onions and ginger and stir-fry for another minute. Combine remaining rice wine, the soy sauce and about $\frac{1}{3}$ cup water and add to chicken along with walnuts. Stir-fry for another minute, make sure chicken is cooked through, and it's ready!

Prep time: 20 minutes
Delicious with: Rice
Calories per serving: 370

Variation:

Chicken with Mustard and Sesame Oil
Prepare chicken breast pieces as described above and stir-fry in the hot oil. Combine 1 heaping tablespoon spicy mustard with $\frac{1}{3}$ cup chicken stock and add. Drizzle with 1 tablespoon sesame oil and serve. You can also include green onions and ginger in the recipe if desired.

141

Peking Duck
Royal cuisine for beginners

Pampers 4:

For the duck:

2 duck breasts with skin (about 12 oz. each)

2 tablespoons molasses

1 heaping teaspoon salt

For the pancakes:

1½ cups flour plus more for working the dough

Sesame oil for frying

For sprinkling and for sauces:

8 green onions

1 small cucumber

¼ cup red bean paste (Asian grocery)

2 teaspoons sesame oil

Plum sauce (bottled, Asian grocery)

1 For duck breasts: About 8 hours ahead of time, boil molasses in ⅓ cup salted water. Place breasts in a bowl, cover with molasses mixture, and let stand 15 minutes. Drain duck but reserve the syrup; let dry with skin side up for about 1 hour. Spread with syrup and let stand for 7 hours, refrigerated.

2 Now for the pancakes: mix together flour and ½ cup lukewarm water, knead briefly and wrap in a damp non-terry towel. Let stand for 20 minutes.

3 Duck breasts: preheat oven to 375°F. Roast duck on middle rack with skin side up for 30 minutes, until the skin is crispy (then reduce heat to 170°F).

4 Meanwhile, remove root ends and any dark green or wilted parts from green onions, rinse rest and cut into 2-inch lengths, then cut into thin strips. Rinse cucumber, halve lengthwise, scrape out seeds and slice rest crosswise thinly.

5 Pancakes: Knead the dough once more and divide into 20 pieces. Roll each piece first into a ball and then into thin rounds on a floured workspace. Brush a hot non-stick pan with a little sesame oil; cook the pancakes one at a time for 1 minute per side. Wrap cooked pancakes in a slightly damp cloth; place in warm oven.

6 Remove duck breasts from oven; slice very thinly. Return to warm oven until serving time. For the sauce, mix bean paste and sesame oil. Pour into individual bowls for serving. Also divide the plum sauce, green onion strips and cucumber slices into individual portions.

7 Transfer duck slices to small plates and serve alongside pancakes. Each guest can: spread a thin layer of one of the sauces on a pancake, top with duck, sprinkle with cucumber or green onions and roll it up.

Prep time: 1 hour
(plus about 8 hours marinating)
Delicious with: Beer or rice wine
Calories per serving: 715

Tip:

In China they always put the whole duck in the oven, but only after it undergoes a special treatment. In order to ensure the skin will be as crisp as parchment after roasting, they massage the duck and pump air between the skin and the meat. This used to be done with a fine straw but is now accomplished with the aid of an air pump. We thought this might be a little too complicated so we invented this simpler version and are extremely satisfied with the results.

Teriyaki Duck
Japanese duck—also delicious served chilled

Feeds 4:

2 duck breasts with the skin (about 10 oz. each)

2–3 leeks

¼ cup sake (Japanese rice wine)

¼ cup mirin (sweet Japanese rice wine)

1 tablespoon sugar

¼ cup soy sauce

2 tablespoons oil

Salt

1 Using a sharp knife, score the skin side of the duck breasts several times in a criss-cross pattern. Remove root ends and any dark green or wilted parts from leeks, slit rest open lengthwise and rinse thoroughly; cut at an angle into ¼-inch slices.

2 Heat a wok or pan and fry duck breast with the skin side down for about 5 minutes until the skin is crispy. Turn and fry for another 2–3 minutes. Remove duck breasts, pour out the fat they produced and return the duck to the pan.

3 Stir together sake, mirin, sugar and soy sauce and pour over the duck breasts. Cover and cook over medium heat for about 5 minutes. Turn duck breasts; cover and cook another 5 minutes. Meanwhile, heat oil in another pan or wok and stir-fry leeks for a few minutes until crisp-tender. Season with salt.

4 Using a sharp knife, cut duck breasts into thin slices and serve alongside leeks.

Prep time: 30 minutes
Delicious with: Rice or Japanese soba or udon noodles, paper-thin daikon radish slices and medium-hot mustard or wasabi
Calories per serving: 440

Red Chicken Curry
Nothing could be easier

Feeds 4:

1⅓ lbs. chicken breasts

½ lb. cherry tomatoes

⅔ cup canned pineapple chunks

2 stalks lemon grass

1 tablespoon oil

1–2 tablespoons red curry paste

1⅔ cups canned coconut milk

1 tablespoon brown sugar

1½ tablespoons fish sauce

2 tablespoons fresh lime juice

A few cilantro leaves for sprinkling

1 Cut chicken into ½-inch cubes. Rinse cherry tomatoes. Drain pineapple in a colander. Rinse lemon grass, trim top and bottom ends, discard/remove outer layer and chop the rest finely.

2 Heat oil in a wok or pan, stir in curry paste and sauté briefly. Add coconut milk and bring to a gentle boil. Add lemon grass, sugar, fish sauce and lime juice. Add chicken and pineapple and simmer uncovered for 5 minutes. Make sure chicken is cooked through—opaque, with no pink remaining.

3 Now just stir in the tomatoes and heat through. Sprinkle on cilantro leaves as a garnish.

Prep time: 20 minutes
Delicious with: Rice and more rice
Calories per serving: 320

143

Swee

Just for you. Let's drink a glass of plum wine to that!

t s

This is just for you. Because Westerners love desserts so much and because sometimes it's hard to find lots of sweets in Asian cuisine, we've searched high and low to come up with a prime selection. There really are some great ones to try: Banana Flambé, Mango Cream, Coconut Flan. It all sounds pretty enticing, doesn't it? Let's drink a glass of plum wine to that!

Finger Exercise No. 7
Mango Porcupines

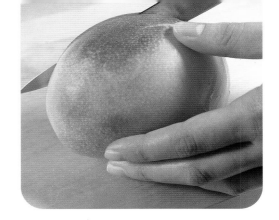

Mastering this exercise will help you cultivate the courage to go to extremes and turn everything upside down.

1. From an unpeeled mango, cut away the two "fruit halves" lengthwise and flat along each side of the pit—set aside to make the porcupines. Peel the fruit that remains on the pit, if desired, to enjoy as your own personal snack. Just be sure to lean over the sink while you eat the fruit away from the pit.

2. Cut a checkerboard pattern into the fruit halves, cutting all the way down to the peel without actually piercing it. It's best to use a table knife because there's no pointy tip.

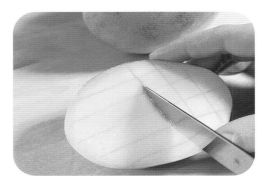

3. Now hold a mango half by the two ends with the peel side down, with your thumbs on the top edge and your fingers below resting on the peel. Gently press up on the peel side and turn the mango half inside-out. Your mango porcupine is ready and can be served "as is" for dessert—or use as a garnish for a fruit or dessert tray. Also, cubes can be cut away from the peel with a very sharp knife to be used in fruit salad.

Sudah makan, Betty?
Let me translate: Have you eaten lunch, Betty? Let me recommend Singapore, the cleanest city in Asia with what must be the best restaurant scene! We live in a shophouse, which is a small hotel that used to be a department store. For breakfast we go to the "kopi tiam," the coffee shop. For lunch we meander through the "hawker center" where food stalls magically appear and prepare Indian, Malaysian and Chinese dishes from every imaginable region. Everything is absolutely authentic! Later we buy something sweet from a Japanese confectionary as well as a kopi (coffee, remember). In the evening we take a crash course in nonya food, which is Asian fusion cooking with a long tradition—prepared in a Chinese style with Indian seasonings and eaten the Malaysian way, with hands and spoons instead of chopsticks. Unbelievably good! But there's also modern fusion cooking, and the places that serve it look as chic as in Chicago except that the flavor is much more authentic. Oops, gotta go, I'm off to the night market to go gnosh on some prawns!

Bye!
Your niece, Margo

To:
Aunt Betty
123 Homesick Lane
Des Moines, Iowa
United States

12.06.2002
POST
Basic Services
5

Homemade Asian Basics
Coconut Milk

What exotic ingredient can be found in the middle of winter on the shelves of even the tiniest small-town grocery store? Dried, grated coconut! Thanks to the coconut macaroon, it has become at least as westernized as bananas. But you can also make it into something truly Asian—coconut milk. The process is a bit time consuming, but rewarding.

Bring 2 cups water to a boil and pour into a bowl containing 3 1/3 cups grated coconut (unsweetened if possible—check health food stores). Let stand for 15 minutes and then process in a blender.

Wrap a bunch of the pulp in a non-terry towel or multiple layers of cheesecloth and wring it out as well as possible into a bowl. Repeat this process until you've squeezed out the entire mixture. Real pros can get 1 2/3 cups liquid out of it. If you let it stand a while, coconut cream forms on the top. The milk below can be used just as you would use canned coconut milk (for a richer affect, stir the coconut cream into the coconut milk).

Also a good idea: Squeeze out the grated coconut a second time for a less intense coconut flavor into soups and sauces.

Drinking Asian Style:
Hard Liquor

As a follow-up to our surprising revelations about beer in the last chapter, here's a liquor shocker: The Asian culture tends not to drink much but when they do, they really go for it. Business people who have been taken out to dinner in China or Japan could tell you stories. Or maybe not, because with an alcohol content of 50% or more, Asia's liquors will erase your memory in no time flat.

China is a little more rustic in its approach than Japan. Since the South grows rice and the North grows grain, the best liquors are distilled in the North. One of these is "moutai," made from wheat and grain sorghum. Even more famous is the millet liquor "kaoling," which really packs a punch with its alcohol content of up to 60%. Even herbal and medicinal spirits have a tradition in China, as do the liqueurs perfumed with blossoms that you can find at some Chinese restaurants.

As for Japan, they have a fine rice liquor called shochu and are more adept at copying Western drinks than the other Asian countries. Suntory whisky, whose distillation is modeled after single-malt scotch, is prized the world over, as is Japanese brandy.

Southeast Asian drinks can range from hearty to intense. Tuak, or toddy, is a wine made from palm syrup that ferments so quickly, tuak poured in the morning has a different flavor from the same tuak poured in the evening. Plus, this drink always needs to be consumed no later than the next day. Whew!

Arrak, another drink, takes everything one step further. It's produced by fermenting tuak, coconut sap or cane sugar with a little rice—which raises the alcohol content. The result tastes like rum and can knock your socks off. Even the natives sometimes prefer to leave it alone.

Crispy Fruit with Cinnamon Yogurt Sauce
Who can resist?

Feeds 4–6:

For the batter:

1 whole green cardamom pod (or a couple pinches of powdered cardamom)

1⅓ cups flour

1 pinch salt

1 tablespoon brown sugar

1 egg

For the fruit:

1 mango

1 banana

1 small pineapple

4 cups oil for deep-frying

For the sauce:

1 cup yogurt

1 teaspoon ground cinnamon

2 tablespoons brown sugar (packed)

A little fresh lemon zest

1 For the batter, crush cardamom very finely in a mortar or dedicated spice grinder. Transfer to a bowl and combine with flour, salt and sugar. Gradually add ⅔ cup water while stirring. Finally, beat in the egg. Cover batter and let stand for about 30 minutes.

2 In the meantime, peel mango, cut the fruit from the pit and cut into bite-size pieces (or use method on page 146 and cut mango away from the peel). Peel banana and slice. Peel pineapple by cutting off exterior with a sharp chef's knife. Cut pineapple lengthwise into quarters, remove core from each and cut into bite-size pieces.

3 Heat oil for deep-frying in a wok or pot. Test the temperature with a wooden spoon: Lower the spoon handle down into the oil and if many tiny bubbles immediately congregate around it, the oil is hot enough. Or, use an oil thermometer, which should register to 350–375°F.

4 Little by little, dunk fruit pieces into the batter (to coat) and then place in the hot oil. Fry in batches until crispy, remove with a slotted metal utensil, drain and place on a paper-towel lined platter.

5 Meanwhile make the dipping sauce by stirring cinnamon, brown sugar and lemon zest into the yogurt. Serve alongside the crispy fruit.

Prep time: 50 minutes
Calories per serving (6): 355

Banana Flambé
Unbelievably tasty!

Feeds 4:

1 lime

1 vanilla bean

6 bananas

3 tablespoons butter

2 tablespoons brown sugar

¼ cup light or dark rum

4 scoops vanilla ice cream

or Coconut Ice Cream (page 154)

1 Rinse lime, pat dry and remove a thin layer of zest (without the white part), either with a zester or vegetable peeler. Just make sure you then cut the zest into very fine strips. Squeeze juice from lime.

2 Slit open vanilla bean lengthwise and scrape out the black seeds with the back of a knife blade. Peel bananas and halve each lengthwise.

3 In a pan large enough for all the banana halves, melt 1 tablespoon of the butter and add the vanilla seeds. Add the bananas and sauté on both sides over medium heat until slightly browned, then remove and set aside, on a platter.

4 Spoon remaining butter into the pan, add brown sugar and stir until everything melts. Add lime zest and then lime juice and simmer for 2–3 minutes.

5 And now let's get down to business— time to flambé! First think about the fact that there are going to be flames, which don't go well with long hair or loose clothing. So make sure anything that might come in contact with the flames is taken care of—and that there's nothing flammable nearby. (Try this recipe at your own risk.) Pour rum into the pan. Light a match, preferably a long one. Tip the pan slightly and hold the match to the surface of the sauce. It should catch fire immediately.

6 When the flames die out (this should happen relatively quickly), place the bananas in the sauce and heat well. They should be served hot, paired with cold ice cream.

Prep time: 20 minutes
Calories per serving: 270

Basic Tip

To make sure all the fruit arrives on the table nice and hot (for the crispy fruit recipe), it's best to keep the finished fruit warm in a 170°F oven until the rest is ready. Don't stack it—lay it out side by side, or else the crispy batter will turn soggy.

Sticky Rice with Mangoes
From Thailand

Feeds 4:

1/2 cup short- or medium-grain rice

1 cup coconut milk

2 tablespoons sugar

1 mango

1 Pour glutinous rice into a bowl, cover well with water and let soak overnight.

2 Drain rice and transfer to a pot. Add about 1 cup water (it should stand about 1/4-inch above the rice) and bring to a boil. Cover and cook rice over very low heat for about 20 minutes until it's tender and has soaked up all the liquid. Let cool.

3 Stir 2 tablespoons coconut milk into the rice. Combine the rest of the milk and the sugar, simmer for 5 minutes and let cool. Peel mango, cut the fruit away from the pit and dice.

4 Heap the sticky rice and mango into wide bowls, pour the sweetened coconut milk over the top of each portion and enjoy!

Prep time: 15 minutes (plus overnight soaking + 20 minutes cooking time)
Calories per serving: 150

Coconut Flan with Pineapple Sauce
Not much work and very impressive

Feeds 6:

For the flan:

3 eggs

1/3 cup sugar

Zest from 1 lime

1 2/3 cups canned coconut milk

1 pinch salt

2 tablespoons light rum

For the sauce:

1 1/4 cups canned pineapple chunks

1 tablespoon sugar

3 tablespoons fresh lime juice

1 pinch ground ginger

Plus:

Butter and grated coconut for the baking dishes

Mint leaves for garnish

1 Coat six small baking dishes (each with a volume of about 2/3 cup) with a little butter and sprinkle with grated coconut. Tilt dishes all around so the sides are well covered with coconut. Pour about an inch of warm water into a 9 x 13-inch baking pan with 2-inch high sides. Place baking dishes in the pan, lowering them down into the water (water should come halfway up the sides of the dishes).

2 Break eggs into a bowl, add sugar and lime zest and beat until foamy. Then add coconut milk, salt and light rum and beat well. Pour the mixture into the baking dishes slowly so the grated coconut remains stuck to the sides.

3 Place the baking pan in the oven (middle rack) and set oven to 300°F. Bake for an hour until the flan is firm. If too much water evaporates, add a little more. If the water begins to boil or bubbles noticably, add cold water.

4 You can either make the sauce now or while the flan is cooling. In any case, drain the pineapple in a colander, being careful to save the juice. Purée pineapple with 2–3 tablespoons of the juice, sugar, lime juice and the ground ginger.

5 When the flan is cool, run a knife blade around the insides of the baking dishes and reverse flans onto small plates. Dress it up with the sauce and fresh mint sprigs.

Prep time: 20 minutes
(plus 1 hour cooking time + cooling time)
Calories per serving: 190

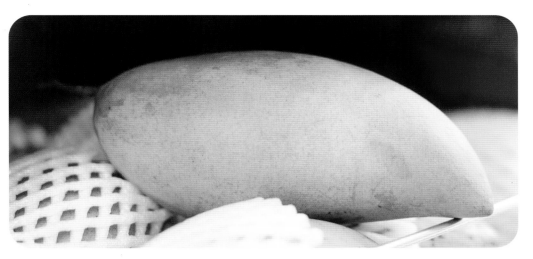

Tropical Tapioca
Sweet, creamy and fruity

Feeds 6:

For the pudding:

5 oz. dry tapioca balls

½ cup brown sugar

1 cup coconut milk

1 pinch salt

For the salad:

1 small pineapple

1 mango

1 papaya

1 banana

8 lychees (canned is fine if fresh

is unavailable)

Juice from 1 lime and 1 orange

Sugar (optional)

1 For the pudding, pour tapioca balls into a bowl and pour on enough cold water to cover the balls. Let stand 1 hour, then drain in a colander, transfer to a pot and cover once again with fresh water. Heat and gently simmer over low heat for 10 minutes.

2 Return tapioca to the colander and rinse under cold water. Place brown sugar, coconut milk and salt in the pot, heat and stir until the brown sugar has dissolved. Stir in tapioca and let cool in the coconut milk. Then transfer to six small dessert-sized glasses and refrigerate until serving.

3 Now for the fruit salad: Peel pineapple using a sharp chef's knife. Cut flesh away from the core, trim any brown spots and dice. Peel mango and cut the fruit from the pit. When it becomes fibrous, don't cut any deeper.

4 Halve the papaya, scoop out the black seeds with a spoon and peel. Peel bananas. Break hard shell off of lychees, cut into the fruit and detach the pits. Cut up all this fruit and mix with the citrus juices. If desired, add sugar to taste. You can either marinate briefly or serve immediately with the pudding.

Prep time: 50 minutes
(plus 1 hour soaking time + cooling time)
Calories per serving: 215

Tip:
Sometimes it's very hard to get exotic ingredients. You can't always find the right fruit and when you do, it can look uninviting. In this case, instead of using unripe mango, papaya and pineapple (they have no flavor!), use canned fruit. Or else decide right away that your dish need not be authentic and leave the exotic fruit for another time. After all, there are other kinds of fruit in the world! Tapioca and coconut milk go just as well with strawberries, figs, plums or raspberries. Don't believe it? Try it and you'll see!

151

Oranges in Syrup
Simply classy!

Feeds 4:

4 oranges

$^2/_3$ cup packed brown sugar

2 teaspoons orange blossom water (gourmet or Mediterranean grocery)

Mint leaves for garnish

1 Cut off a thick layer of orange peel around the whole orange with a very sharp knife, making sure to rid of all the white membrane. Then cut out the exposed segments using the knife, from between the inner section walls. Place in a bowl. Finally, squeeze the remaining orange halves and collect the juice, along with the juice you produced by cutting out the segments.

2 In a pot, heat brown sugar and $^2/_3$ cup water. Bring to a boil and simmer over medium heat for about 10 minutes until it becomes a syrupy consistency. Stir in the fresh-squeezed orange juice and continue simmering briefly. Then let syrup cool until lukewarm.

3 Fan out orange segments on small plates or in small bowls. Stir orange blossom water into the brown sugar syrup and drizzle over the orange segments. Garnish with fresh mint leaves or sprigs and serve.

Prep time: 30 minutes
Delicious with: Coconut or Passion Fruit Ice Cream (both on page 154) or with cookies
Calories per serving: 175

Basic Tip

No matter how simple the dessert, sprinkling on a few fresh herbs will give it a professional look. It's usually easy enough to find fresh herbs at your local grocery store, such as mint—but it's not always easy to keep them fresh for when you want to use them. So why not plant some herb seeds, including mint, in some pots and keep them in your windowsill. Keep them watered, make sure they're getting some sunlight, and you'll always have fresh herbs on hand.

Coconut Ice Milk
Simply delicious!

Feeds 6:

1 lime

1 vanilla bean

²/₃ cup sugar

1²/₃ cups canned coconut milk

Grated coconut for sprinkling

1 Rinse lime well, pat dry and grate off the zest. Squeeze juice from lime. Slit open vanilla bean lengthwise and scrape out the black seeds with the back of a knife blade tip.

2 Pour sugar into a pot and heat on low until it turns to liquid, stirring constantly so it melts evenly. Add coconut milk and bring to a gentle boil.

3 Stir in lime zest, lime juice and vanilla bean seeds and let cool to lukewarm. Then transfer mixture to a metal bowl and keep in the freezer for about 3 hours.

4 In the meantime, periodically take the bowl out of the freezer and stir the mixture thoroughly. This will cause it to freeze much more evenly and the ice crystals won't be as large.

5 Remove the ice milk from the freezer about 15 minutes before serving so it won't be too hard. Transfer to bowls using an ice cream scoop. Sprinkle with grated coconut.

Prep time: 20 minutes (plus 3 hours freezing time + 15 minutes thawing time)
Delicious with: Tropical fruit from the Tropical Tapioca recipe (page 151) or any fresh fruit, especially mango or pineapple)
Calories per serving: 100

Passion Fruit Ice Cream
Simply exquisite!

Feeds 6:

1 orange

1 lime

6–8 passion fruit (about 1 lb.)

4 egg whites

¹/₂ cup sugar

¹/₂ cup heavy cream

1 Rinse orange and lime well and pat dry. Grate off a very thin layer of zest and chop finely. Then squeeze juice from orange and lime.

2 Cut passion fruit in half crosswise and spoon out fruit, including seeds (save shells). In a clean and dry bowl, beat egg whites until stiff, while slowly adding sugar towards the end of the process.

3 Beat cream until stiff peaks form. Stir together whipped cream, passion fruit, citrus peel and citrus juice. Fold in stiff egg whites, transfer to a metal bowl and place in the freezer. It takes 4–5 hours for the ice cream to solidify. Periodically, remove from the freezer and stir mixture—this will help it to freeze more evenly.

4 Take the ice cream out of the freezer a little ahead of time so it won't be too hard— about 15 minutes before serving. Shape into balls with an ice cream scoop and, if you want, serve it in the half-shells from the passion fruit. (Do not serve this dish to young children, the elderly, or anyone with a compromised immune system, as it contains raw egg whites.)

Prep time: 25 minutes (plus 4–5 hours freezing time + 15 minutes thawing time)
Delicious with: Whipped cream with a little rum in it
Calories per serving. 145

154

Melon in Coconut Milk
Quickly made, quickly eaten

Makes enough for 4:

1 cantaloupe

1 vanilla bean

Zest of ½ lime

1 ¾ cup coconut milk

¼ cup sugar

2 tablespoons light rum

1 Cut open melon in half crosswise. Scoop out seeds with a spoon, and then peel and dice the fruit. Or, even better—use a melon baller.

2 Slit open vanilla bean and scrape out seeds using the back of a knife blade tip. Rinse lime and remove zest from half, taking care to not get any of the white pith (which is bitter). Combine zest and vanilla bean seeds with coconut milk and sugar, bring to a gentle boil and stir until the sugar dissolves. Let cool. Whisk rum into the mixture and then add melon pieces. Let refrigerate for at least 1 hour. Great with Pacific Rim meals!

Prep time: 20 minutes
(+ 1 hour refrigeration time)
Calories per serving: 135

Tip:
Experiment with this recipe by trying different varieties of melon or even fruits such as mango or papaya—you can even use a melon baller on these fruits. Also, try different liqueurs in place of the light rum.

Mango Cream
Simply fast!

Feeds 4:

1 very ripe mango (ripeness is important; otherwise it won't purée as well)

1 cup canned coconut milk

⅓ cup sugar

1 tablespoon fresh lime juice

A little ground cardamom

1 Peel mango and cut the fruit away from the pit. Finely purée mango, coconut milk and sugar using a blender, hand blender or food processor.

2 Season purée to taste with lime juice, transfer to small bowls and refrigerate for 1 hour or more. Then dust very lightly with cardamom and it's ready!

Prep time: 10 minutes (plus 1 hour—or more—of refrigeration time)
Calories per serving: 110

Index

Credits

The Authors:

Sebastian Dickhaut, text pages

Cornelia Schinharl, recipe pages

Kelsey Lane, American team editor

Photography:
Germany and U.S. teams

Rice bowl on title page: Eising FoodPhotography, Martina Görlach

Barbara Bonisolli: All recipe photos and various still-life photos – Back cover (bottom left, top right); 17 Basic Flavors pages 12–13; 17 Handy Items pages 28–29; feature photos on theory pages 16, 17, 24 (bottom), 25, 26 (right), 27 (bottom); photos for finger exercises pages 38, 56, 74, 88, 108, 126, 146; feature photos on recipe pages 47 (right), 62 (right), 67 (center), 83 (right), 85 (right), 101 (right), 112 (center), 113 (right), 119 (left), 120 (center), 131 (left), 133 (left), 137 (right), 140 (center), 141 (left), 143 (center), 152, 155 (center)

Alexander Walter: People and action photos except those provided by Lisa Keenan noted below, products in Asian market and various still-life photos—motif on outside flap; back cover (bottom right); photo on contents page 2; two-page opening pages 4–5 and 34–35; feature photos on theory pages 6, 8, 9, 18, 19, 20, 21, 22, 24 (top), 26 (left), 27 (top), 32; opening pages for all recipe sections; feature photos on recipe pages 41, 42 (center), 44, 47 (left), 50 (center), 51 (right), 53 (right), 59, 61 (center), 63 (right), 64, 66 (center), 70 (right), 78 (center), 79 (left), 82 (center), 83 (left), 85 (left), 91, 93 (right) 96 (center), 97 (left), 98 (right), 99 (right), 101 (left), 104 (center), 105 (left, right), 111, 115 (left, right), 116, 119 (right), 122, 129, 131 (right), 132 (center), 136 (center), 138, 141 (right), 149, 151 (right), 154 (center)

Lisa Keenan: 23, 33 (center), 43 (left), 121 (left), 137 (left), back cover (lower right)

iPUBLISH GmbH, GANSKE INTERACTIVE PUBLISHING: Map on inside front flap

Thank you to:
Suzanne Bergfelder who allowed us to use her apartment for this photo shoot.
John Ly and the women of the Munich Hong Kong Market who allowed us to take photos of their skyscrapers of soy sauce and hills of hundred-year eggs.
Tamayo Funami who initiated us into the art of everyday sushi.
Susanne Bodensteiner who cast an expert eye on texts and recipes.

German Team:
Managing editor: Birgit Rademacker
Concept and idea: Sebastian Dickhaut, Cornelia Schinharl, Sabine Sälzer
Editor: Sabine Sälzer (also production)
Design (and set/DTP): Christina Kempe
Layout: Sybille Engels, Thomas Jankovic
Production: Susanne Mühldorfer
Copyediting: Redaktionsbüro
Photography: Barbara Bonisolli (food), Alexander Walter (people)
Photographer's assistants: Claudia Juranits, Florian Peljak
Food stylist: Hans Gerlach
Photo requisitioning/styling: Christa Schmedes, Sebastian Dickhaut
Models: Annika Möller, Markus Röleke, Janna Sälzer, Gabi Schnitzlein
Final corrections: Mischa Gallé
Repro: Repro Ludwig
Printing and binding: Druckhaus Kaufmann

U.S. Team:
Editor: Kelsey Lane
Translator: Christie Tam
Production: Patty Holden
Copy editing: Elizabeth Penn
Photography: Lisa Keenan (food, people)

Thank you to Bob Lane for helping with index preparation.

Published originally under the title ASIAN BASICS: Alles, was man braucht fürs yin und yang in der Küche.
© 2002 Gräfe und Unzer Verlag, GmbH, Munich

English translation copyright: © 2003 Silverback Books

ISBN: 1-930603-65-7

Printed in Hong Kong